The Gospel
According to
Superman

The Gospel According to Superman

by John T. Galloway, Jr.

A. J. HOLMAN COMPANY
Division of J.B. Lippincott Company
Philadelphia and New York

Unless otherwise noted, the scripture quotations in this publication are from the Revised Standard Version of the Bible, copyrighted 1946 and 1952 by the Division of Christian Education of the National Council of Churches of Christ in the U.S.A., and used by permission.

The Superman comic strip sequences are reprinted by permission of National Periodical Publications, Inc.

U.S. Library of Congress Cataloging in Publication Data

Galloway, John T
    The gospel according to superman.

    1. Christian life—Presbyterian authors.
2. God. 3. Superman (Comic strip)
I. Title.
BV4501.2.G3   248'.48'51   73–1929
ISBN–0–87981–021–1

*To the members and friends
of the Ogden Presbyterian Church
for their ministry to me in 1968–1972*

Contents

Preface

The Gospel According to Superman strikes a theme quite different from a similar-sounding title of an outstanding book about Peanuts. It is not my intent in this book to find the gospel in Superman. Rather I seek to find the gospel where it can best be found—in scripture and in the changed lives of Christians. That gospel is then compared with the philosophy implicit in the comic strip Superman.

We are living in a time when many man-made philosophies are passing for the Word of Life. It is an age of relativism—"do your own thing"; "believe whatever you want about whatever you want." It is not an age when people want to seek the precise revelation of God so much as to play upon vague wishes.

It has occurred to me that, since the character Superman is an apt example of our human dreams and wishes for a god (with small g), we can see in him how our human philosophies compare with God's revelation. We discover that in some things our God actually inspires our dreams and our projected hero has some things in

common with God. But in the main, since the source is
different, so is the message. God comes to us on His
terms, not ours. He does what is right from His perspective, not ours. He is the Lord, and we are His
people.

The book divides into two sections. The first draws
some implications from our contemporary situation, in-
vestigating how much we need Biblical revelation, and
how out of step it is with the secular mind. The second
section offers us several exercises to sharpen our awareness of how human philosophy and divine revelation are
in tension with each other.

The conception of the book has had three phases. It
began in a seminary classroom when the professor asked
us, as an assignment in his course on educational psy-
chology, to write a term paper on a personality change
found somewhere in literature. Half as a joke I offered
to write on Clark Kent. I received a number of laughs
for the idea. But the more I thought about it, the more
I liked it. I wrote on Clark Kent, and happily the professor liked it too.

Next I developed a short manuscript setting a similar
theme to that of the present book, but with more em-
phasis on social action and the revolution against God
out there. In 1969 I dropped the project.

As a direct outgrowth of the Leighton Ford Crusade
in Rochester in the spring of 1972, I picked up the
theme again but with a completely new and, I feel,
fresh spiritual perspective. The present manuscript is
the result.

I would like to thank Professor James Loder, who
encouraged me to write a term paper that planted the

seed in my mind. The late Clayton "Bud" Collyer was most helpful to me in long discussions about the background of Superman and the experience of his own biblical faith. My tireless secretary, Jean Schult, translated my writing into type. I would like to thank my father, Dr. John T. Galloway, Sr., for his constant nudges in the direction of the pen. And a special thank-you goes to my wife, Susan, who patiently understood me while I was writing.

I cannot refute the rumor that I owe much of the research to a misspent youth reading comics and going to Saturday matinees.

JOHN T. GALLOWAY, JR.

York, Pa.
December, 1972

Part One

1

Look Who's Back!

Superman is alive and well!

In fact I find it rather difficult to pick up a magazine in which he, or some takeoff of him, is not prominently displayed, advertising this product or that. My four-year-old son can recognize him instantly, and he wonders if Superman was around when Daddy was a boy. Yes, son, he was. But I am a bit surprised at how much he is around today.

Frankly, I had feared the worst. I was one of those unbelievers who assumed that the Man of Steel had gone the way of the Edsel, the twist, and Baby Snooks, may they rest in peace. With a twinge of sadness I recalled the radio beside my bed twenty years ago challenging my imagination with verbal pictures: "Look! Up in the sky! It's a bird! It's a plane! It's Superman!" Or what of those Saturday afternoon matinees? I used to get in for fourteen cents. Can you believe that? Flash Gordon would alternate with serials of Superman, and we could hardly wait for the next week to roll around so we could see how Superman would get out of some catastrophic dilemma. But today a few gray hairs are here; and Superman is not. At least that is what I thought.

For a while he *was* gone. But now he is back. Perhaps the new nostalgia boom brought on his resurrection. Television commercials are featuring old three-story village houses as abodes for the happy family that uses the right product. Movie makers are tugging at the heartstrings of a generation that was fifteen in the *Summer of '42*. Disc jockeys on pop record stations find that simply playing and replaying the top ten is not enough for the nostalgic listener. Golden oldies are regularly featured, and some stations dedicate entire weekends to the history of rock and roll. Even the top ten tunes smack of revival time, as modern artists simply remake old songs. On college campuses and at cocktail parties people pass hours in the seemingly senseless but captivating game of trivia. What was the name of Gene Autry's horse? What was the name of Our Miss Brooks's school? Who lived next door to Ozzie and Harriet? Trivia, to be sure. But more than that, it is replaying those good old days. There is, at least in this sense, some Archie Bunker in us all. Ah, yes! Those were the days.

Amid all of the returning to those thrilling days of yesteryear, Superman has come back, along with the impulsively naïve Jimmy Olsen, the lady-in-waiting Lois Lane, and "Great Caesar's Ghost" Perry White, and to round out the cast we have our hero's alter ego, Clark Kent, along with a few bad guys.

A closer look reveals that more is going on in Superman's return than a simple desire to replay an old sensation. He is the kind of folk hero who speaks very clearly, very poignantly to our day. In him we can see joined together the dreams and hopes, the cynicism and mockery, the facts and illusions of the modern mind. He is back because he is timely.

Most of the bits and pieces of nostalgia are flocking back in much the same packages in which we received them years ago: radio and TV shows, records, movies, or magazines. But the Man of Steel is back in new forms. Linda Sunshine has compiled an anthology of Superman comics entitled *Superman: From the Thirties to the Seventies.* That is about the only way we receive the old medium of comics. I may buy an old Buddy Holly album, but I won't buy an old Superman comic book. Comics are still available, but I don't buy them. The Saturday matinee is past. Superman is not regularly on network TV or radio.

Where then is he? He is deeply embedded in our collective mind, repeatedly showing himself in unexpected places: the theater, commercials, casual conversation. He is a part of our cultural mind as an image, an idea to be used. And it is being used. I don't need to buy a comic to see Superman. I just need to look around me.

Walking on a city street not long ago, I passed a character whose attire has become almost commonplace. He was expressing his individuality in the same way as so many others his age. Charles Reich has pointed out from his observations of young people that kids today dress not according to social convention but according to how they feel, who they think they are, what identity they want to portray. That insight flashed into my mind as this particular young man passed me on the sidewalk. He was wearing a somewhat ragged but still recognizable Superman sweat shirt. There across his chest was the well-known insignia. A put-on, perhaps; but he put on the shirt for a reason. I suspect quite a bit goes on in the life of a young man facing the world from behind the red "S" of Superman.

What brought me almost to a halt was not the sweat shirt alone; I have seen them on magazine covers, hanging in shops around town, and even at church. But I was not prepared for the composite impression made on me by this fellow. There, in a Superman get-up, was the spitting image of Jesus, the carpenter's son from Nazareth. He too is back in what I hope is more than a nostalgia boom. At crusades and revivals, it is young people who are filling up the audience. Jesus is in. This fellow had the exact look about him that I have seen hundreds of times in a frame on a Sunday school wall: the brown eyes, the gentle, meek, and mild posture—*in a Superman sweat shirt!* I could not believe it.

For a while, it made no sense. This younger generation seems hopelessly fouled up, I thought. How can anyone confuse the powerful steel hero with the meek suffering servant? The head of Jesus atop a Superman suit is a silly, almost blasphemous image. But blasphemy is a very difficult subject to discuss these days —it being so commonplace. Perhaps there is advantage in that. People are freer to express their insights. That young man may be onto something valid and valuable. In his honesty he may be saying what is so very real but so hidden in our culture. There *is* a link between our dream hero, Superman, and our God-given Savior, Jesus Christ, a link that we need to analyze if our faith is to be clarified and deepened.

When the director of the off-Broadway musical *Godspell* set about the business of selecting costumes for the characters, what did he choose? The play is about the teachings of Jesus; there is festive, carnival atmosphere about it. How did he dress Jesus? You guessed it. He appears in a Superman sweat shirt, with that big red "S" standing out for all to see.

It sounds odd to be saying this, but I firmly believe there is a parabolic message for all of us in the simultaneous reemergence of two men whose lives and messages dovetail at odd angles into what we so nonchalantly call faith and values.

2

Whence Cometh Our Hero?

Evolutionists may or may not be right about the long history of mankind. But they certainly would have a strong case regarding the chronicle of Superman. In a commercial world where it is only the fittest that survive, the character Superman has risen to great fame that has been sustained through several decades of marked change in Western culture. Superman has adapted to that change steadily and surely.

Back in the days when America was regaining her feet after the Depression, and Adolf Hitler was a curious maniac some still hoped to appease, folks used to enjoy sitting on their porches waiting for the mail train, properly awed by the powerful locomotive speeding past. The new hero that emerged in comic strips was described as "faster than a locomotive." Brother, that was movin'!

But quiet pastoral scenes gave way to the mayhem of war. Now guns were the thing. An enemy soldier was spotted two hundred yards across a field, a shot was fired, and barely had the sound begun to crash upon the eardrum when the enemy was seen toppling to the ground. Naturally any hero who intended to keep up with the times had to meet some new criteria. Superman was certainly going to keep up with the times. In adapting to new demands, he became "faster than a speeding bullet." In deference to the good old train engine, which now seemed rather slow in comparison, our hero became *"more powerful* than a locomotive."

War had its impact. It was said of Superman that "nothing less than a bursting shell could penetrate his skin." By war's end he was able to withstand even an atomic bomb. Later, he acquired X-ray vision. Needless to say, in the present age of astronauts, he has gone interplanetary to keep up his fight for "truth, justice, and the American way," though some of the lead-ins to Superman episodes recently seem to have deleted the "American way." This too may be a sign of the times.

Any theory of evolution worth its salt must inspire some speculation about where it all began. Where did Superman begin? Tracing him back through time we notice that the farther back we go the less spectacular his feats become. This might lead us to assume he began as plain old everyday Joe Doaks on Main Street. The idea is not without foundation. Superman himself, appearing in comic books, has always been blessed with qualities no average mortal possessed. But his origin is tied to Joe Doaks in the sense that Joe dreams him up, identifies with him, and projects his wishes into him.

From the beginning there has been a tie between

Superman and the average man. When the character first appeared in the June issue of *Action Comics* in 1938 it was obvious that something of significance was occurring. By the following year Superman had his own magazine. He was a regular in newspapers. And the year after that radio listeners first heard, "Look! Up in the sky! It's a bird! It's a plane! It's Superman!" The Mutual Broadcasting System made Superman a permanent fixture, with the late Clayton "Bud" Collyer of *Beat the Clock* and *To Tell the Truth* fame doing the voices of Superman and Clark Kent.

It was my great good fortune to have known Mr. Collyer and to have talked with him at length about the character who helped launch his career. At the time of our conversations in 1967, Bud was not only taping *To Tell the Truth,* he was also doing the voice for an animated cartoon series of his old friend Superman.

According to Mr. Collyer, Superman was born during a college bull session. Two students in an eastern university were batting the breeze one day about the imaginary heroes little kids dream up to make them feel secure or important. As one young man began to go into some detail about a certain personality that kept reappearing in his own youthful fantasizing, the other realized that this character bore striking similarities to one in his own dreams. The wheels turned. If such a dream hero was common to the two of them, perhaps in some fashion it was similar to the dreams of other kids. Would youngsters everywhere be interested in reading about such a marvelous champion of justice? One of the students began to do some sketches while the other worked out scenarios, and before long they had a hero ready to go to market.

Their assumptions proved right. People did want to read of Superman, to hear about him, and to see him. This was a hero who had lived in vague form within their dreams. Now their dreams, their projections, were out where they could be seen and be given common acceptance.

To say that Superman came into being because people thought him up is to say nothing at all. Obviously people thought him up. More important to our discussion is the apparent fact that Superman represents an expression of basic natural human impulses at work in the world of wish. Little boys dream of such things. Not-so-little boys do too, in much more grown-up ways, of course. Superman is what people want, what they wish existed. He is a hero with a direct link to the inner world. When people allow their minds to drift, as little children often do, they find images of their saving hero and ethical ideal. The evidence is that the common qualities of such projected dreams are to be found in Superman.

The evolutionist has a point. Superman *can* be traced back to the common man. He has an origin in you and me.

3

God Comparisons

A nagging question crops up at this point. If Superman is really a figment of human imaginings, a symbol of what people fantasize in coping with life, is there not a chilling piece of bad news for us when Superman is portrayed so much like God? Memories of those living-room discussion groups from high school and college days flash back. If someone isn't pestering the leader with questions about the people in Africa who have not heard of Jesus (will they get into heaven?), someone else is insisting that God is a being cooked up by adults to help them preserve order and face death. Have we not torpedoed all this faith business when we can show that God is really a spiritual model of a comic-book character? Haven't we proved God is just another dreamed-up hero?

Not really. But the comparison is nonetheless worth pursuing.

Every year *Esquire* magazine in a hilarious section makes awards for oddities that occurred during the previous year. We read of such outstanding misfortunes as the hunter who accidentally shot himself in the leg. Being alone, he knew that he had to summon help. He fired another shot, hoping to catch someone's attention, and in so doing shot himself in the other leg. An award-winning performance! A preacher found himself so honored a few years back. He won a spot in the pages of *Esquire* for preaching a sermon in which he said that God is a lot like Superman, swooping down from the heavens to straighten things out in human life and then—"Up, up, and away!"—ascending again to the great beyond.

Call the award what you will, the preacher was at least right about one thing. Without wanting to take Superman too seriously, one can find an extraordinarily high number of points of comparison between the Superman of the comics and the God revealed in scripture and in the person of Jesus Christ. On the surface of it, the comparison seems almost complete.

Fighting a never-ending battle for "truth, justice, and the American way," the purposes of the Man of Steel and of God appear the same. Both intervene in time of trouble. Rather than being able to walk on water, change water into wine, or pass through locked doors, Superman is described as "faster than a speeding bullet, more powerful than a locomotive, able to leap tall buildings at a single bound." He is indeed "a strange visitor from another planet who came to earth with powers and abilities far beyond those of mortal men." He is the power from beyond in the midst of Metropolis, a characteristic that must send chills up and down the spines of theologians who so passionately describe Christ as "the beyond in our midst" and their comrades who insist that God lives in the city. Even a dash of old-time Calvinism can be thrown in. Superman has his chosen elect: Jimmy Olsen, Lois Lane, and Perry White. After reading only one episode it is quite clear that all things work together for good for those who love Superman and who are called according to his purpose. And why not? He can change the course of mighty rivers and would have little trouble separating the waters of the Red Sea. He can bend steel in his bare hands and would find it a cinch to break open jail doors when New Testament writers were held captive. When the editors of *Esquire* cited the preacher's sermon, they said that it sounded odd. But they were not denying that the good dominie had a point.

What we are talking about in this chapter is God comparison. It is a topic that can have a very odd feel, as God comparison runs the gamut from illumination to blasphemy. The shades of gray that lie between often leave us quite uneasy. Perhaps the preceding paragraph is a case in point. The Superman-God parallel is in many ways making a revelation. Yet it is blasphemous in much of its tone.

Since this book is really an exercise in God comparison, a bit of clarification of the subject might be helpful.

There are four models for making a God comparison.

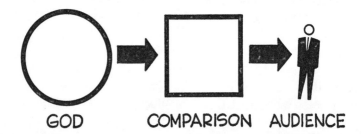

GOD   COMPARISON AUDIENCE

In the first we have a fairly vivid picture of who God is and what he is about. But we need some way to get this great truth across to our audience. Often we simply have so much awareness of God's fullness and presence that words alone fail to do justice. Just as a picture is worth a thousand words, so is a verbal image. Jesus was a master at this technique, painting many verbal images in the form of the parables that he told the crowds. (God is like a shepherd searching for the lost sheep; God is like a father waiting for his prodigal son to return.) Using this same strategy for God comparisons is in the best style of Jesus. The preacher uses it in prayerfully searching for the right illustration to help his congregation see the truth that will set them free. Robert Short used the comic strip *Peanuts* to bring the gospel message to millions. The Spirit of the living God is at work in comparisons of this sort.

In our second model we see how important it is to have already made a decision about who the Lord of life really is. Comparison borders on blasphemy when God is not the Truth to be told, the Lord before whom to bow. In this model something less than God is elevated by cloaking it in the likeness of our God. I can

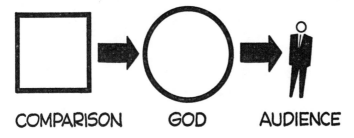

COMPARISON   GOD   AUDIENCE

make something or someone look better if I use godly qualities in the description.

It is done often. One glaring example is taken here from the field of political writing, where candidates are frequently put on donkeys and pointed toward Bethlehem. In 1959 Earl Mazo penned these lines about Richard Nixon:

> Nixon has managed to stand out in one way or another for a good part of his life. He was the first child born in Yorba Linda, a farming village thirty miles inland from Los Angeles. (Next day there was a partial eclipse of the sun.) Nixon's father, whose wide-ranging talents included carpentry, built the family homestead alone, except for the fireplace.

A novel birth in a rustic pastoral setting, son of a carpenter, born at a time when celestial phenomena were occurring—one might have expected to find the babe wrapped in swaddling clothes and lying in a manger. Such comparisons would seem to be using God to make some other point.

The third model is happily common to our culture. Here a story is to be told, not necessarily intending to make any religious statement or to elevate any particular point of view. Almost by accident a message

GOD AND COMPARISON IN UNION

from God comes in. Charles Dickens writes *A Christmas Carol*. On Sesame Street the characters all line up to

march and one insists upon being at the front, only to
be frustrated when the march begins with an "about
face" order and he finds himself last. We recall Jesus'
words, "The first shall be last." The message of the
Judeo-Christian tradition is so deeply ingrained in
Western culture that it almost naturally sprouts up
here or there in our creative expression. The thoughts
of scripture come alive in the secular setting, and the
two become one.

The fourth model is one in which the message of
God is simply not understood. When one thinks of
God, one is really thinking not of God at all but of
popular religion. There are a number of ways this
model could be set up. For our purposes only one is

GOD

POP GOD AND COMPARISON
IN FASCINATION

included. The real message of God is cut off, and
instead the fascination is with a comparison between
some character or object and the god of pop religion.

It is the contention of this book that Superman is a
hero in the public mind because he is compared with
God in a combination of models three and four. To be
sure, any hero in the Western world can in one way
or another be aligned with some aspect of the Judeo-
Christian tradition. When a preacher spots godly qualities in the work of Superman, he illustrates how the
biblical message does appear in some strange places.

At the same time one of the insidious, subtle forces at work challenging the biblical message is pop religion, which also finds itself being expressed in a wide variety of art forms.

If people dreamed up Superman, the same can be said of any god of pop religion. That young fellow at the discussion group insisting that people invented God to take care of their own needs is at least half right. He is dead wrong about those who have encountered the living Christ. But he is quite right about those who drift along on the waves of popular sentiment and the fickle religion that goes along with it.

A teen-ager was in my office one afternoon, chatting about his love life, which was not going very well for him. He had a crush on a girl in another class. The symptoms were all there: loss of appetite, inability to concentrate, weak all over, unable to sleep at night yet dozing during the day, frantic reading into her every gesture some hidden meaning (she loves me; she loves me not). He dreamed about her all the time. But, he said, when he was with her she acted in a funny way. "She isn't really being herself. She isn't acting as I know she should." Sometimes that is a perceptive insight that people can have into each other's lives. But just as often, as in this case, dreams give an image of a person that is untrue. This young fellow dreamed of a girl who was all of the things he wanted. He was desperately in love with his dreams. Alas, he had never really come to know the lovely girl herself.

We do the same thing to God. We are ardent in our faith and devotion before the throne of our deified dreams. But in this age of biblical illiteracy, when our

Bibles are almost never opened, how can we be so arrogant as to claim we really know God? In what ways are we taking the time in our lives to get over our private feelings and shake hands with the God who is waiting to be known?

The Superman-God comparison can be helpful to us in two ways: (1) we can delight in how the Judeo-Christian tradition is expressed in comic art forms; also, (2) since we know that Superman is the product of human dreamings, the expression of human wish projection, and that Superman bears striking resemblance to the god of popular religion, what a tremendous opportunity we have to hold him and his pop god look-alike up to the light of scripture and see what we can discover.

4

Dream On

The dreamer dreamed three nights in succession of seeing a pool of dark water with leaves floating in it, and under the leaves a body. On the third day she was working in her kitchen and with no reason at all, she ran across three front yards into a neighbor's yard, and there it was; an abandoned fish pond and in it a body, floating under dead leaves. It was the body of her small son! Thanks to the dream which her inner being understood even though her outer consciousness did not, she reached him in time and he was saved by artificial respiration and suffered no harm. Had she not been warned by God in a dream, her son would have drowned. On the other hand, if she had known someone who could have helped her interpret the dream, she could have seen to it that the pond was protected by barbed wire or in some other way and her son would not have fallen into it at all.

This is but one of many such illustrations employed by John A. Sanford in his book *Dreams: God's Forgotten Language.* The point Mr. Sanford is making is that dreams are to be taken seriously as a medium through which God conveys a message to mankind. The early church father Tertullian once remarked, "Almost the greater part of mankind derive their knowledge of God from dreams." Certainly the most hasty reading of our Bibles leaves little doubt in our minds that dreams often revealed most urgent messages from God to his people. Joseph was informed in a dream that his fiancée, Mary, who was pregnant, had been singled out by the Holy Spirit to give birth to the Messiah. Later, Joseph was again instructed in a dream to take the baby into Egypt so that the king would not be able to carry out his scheme to have the child murdered.

It would seem that we have run into a snag, or at least a complication, in our thinking. If Superman is the product of human dreams, and if God reveals himself in dreams, we would appear to be on thin ice in calling this Superman dream into question theologically.

This essay is frankly based on certain assumptions about what Tertullian said. If, in claiming "Almost the greater part of mankind derive their knowledge of God from dreams," he was intending to say that most people worship a deity produced in their own dreams, he is quite right. Most folks do seem to have a God (or god) well suited to what we might imagine their dreams to offer.

If, on the other hand, he was claiming that God's most frequently used method of revealing himself is human dreaming, and that the dreams of the majority give us our best image of God, Tertullian would seem to be wrong. For one thing, the god produced by the dreams of the majority has little resemblance to the God of scripture. When a choice has to be made, the bias of this writer comes down on the side of scripture. Further, the record of dreams both in scripture and in history has been that dreams are unique and the gifts are given in particular situations to particular individuals. Joseph had a dream. The mother of a little boy who almost drowned had a dream three nights in a row. But there is no reason to believe that the fusion of all dreams produced by today's Christians would give us a helpful image of our God. We might gain fantastic data for a sociology of the modern church; there might be few instances of godly insight; but they would just as probably be matched by material for an X-rated movie. A reading of church history underscores the fact that indeed God has come to some people in their dreams. But he has reached by far the most through other means.

The witness of the Bible is that you and I have become separated from God. We are living apart from him. It is at the deepest level of our lives that this separation is felt, deep within where we decide who is really going to run our lives. The decision Adam and Eve made, and the decision you and I make day after day, is "I am." We want to be lord of our lives. The dreams we dream, our projections, our wishes come from that inner chamber where our own best interests come first. For this reason the images that emerge from within us need refinement. They need to be challenged.

Superman is the product of human wishes. The God

and Father of Jesus Christ comes from the other side and confronts us with a message that is challengingly new.

There is cause to celebrate the reawakened interest in dreams. As Mr. Sanford states, we have forgotten that God can come to us in our sleep. When he comes we must be prepared to listen. But amid celebration let's not go overboard. We are still mortals whose inner voice tends to be a selfish one. Unless the reader is quite unlike the writer, I think we can agree that the central thrust of our adventures in dreamland is something less than theological. As a general rule of thumb, we are on firmer turf looking outside ourselves to discover our Creator.

5

God and the Gut

I cannot recall if I had just begun my ministry or was only staying with a family in the parish I was first to serve. At any rate, the upstairs bedroom had a most comfortable bed in it and I was taking full advantage of a chance to catch up on my sleep. Something interrupted. Sensing that I might not be alone in the room, I opened one eye and looked right into the bright wide-awake eyes of a five-year-old girl standing in the doorway.

"Hi," she said. It was roughly 6:30 A.M., an absurd hour under the best of circumstances. "Are you going to get up now?" Frankly I had hoped that I would not be getting up. But the smell of bacon and coffee rising from the kitchen suggested I should.

"You run downstairs and help Mommy get breakfast ready, and I'll get dressed."

"I'd rather stay up here and watch you get dressed." Well, I happen to be one of those odd ducks who freely admits to having socially imposed inhibitions and hang-ups. Except for locker rooms and family chambers, I maintain an air of privacy.

"I am sure your mommy needs you downstairs. I do not want you up here while I am getting dressed, and I am sure Mommy doesn't either."

"I'll go ask her if it's okay," said my friend, scampering off downstairs. I was saved . . . or so I thought. But even though Mommy's voice was clear as a bell telling the little girl to stay downstairs, my adventures were not over. I had closed my eyes for that last wink when I sensed again I had company. My pal was back with a great piece of argument.

"Mommy says it is not okay for me to stay up here. You say it is not okay. But I say it's okay. So I'll stay."

Therein lies what may be one of the clearest examples to date of much that travels under the title of modern morality. As a recent hit record chanted over and again, "If it feels good it's all right." We are living in a day when external authorities have lost their impact. People seem increasingly to act not on the basis of what they are instructed to do but on the basis of what they want to do. Even the best efforts of church folk to arrive at a sensitive and sensible kind of new morality run amuck. In an effort to liberate Christians from narrow legalism, the writings of new moralists simply heap more coals on the fire already lit by those who want only to do as they very well please. "So what if Mommy says I can't do it? So what if the man upstairs says no? If I want to stand in the doorway, I will. So there!"

Superman and the false god with whom he so closely compares are products of our inner selves. Man has thought them up. In a day and age when our inner feelings and desires and expressions are so very important, we are going against the current to suggest that our faith needs to be clarified and disciplined by biblical revelation. "I've got my own God. Everybody has his own religion. Don't bore me with all those sterile doctrines and God comparisons." We are up against it when we suggest that projection of personal wishes and dreams is not enough. We are not in keeping with the times to suggest that we need to encounter a power outside us and beyond us, able to change us.

Certainly the momentum is going the other way.

Young people take LSD and other illegal drugs to expand their minds so as to get at those corners of their brains hidden from them by years of social conditioning; adults aim at the same goal legally, taking medication, coffee, alcohol in hopes of really being themselves.

Divinity school students harp about how theology must get off the bookshelf and into everyday life. They are agreed that religion has no impact when it comes to a person through external media. Somehow it has to be real at the "gut level." (For a time on seminary campuses, one could utter all kinds of gibberish, but if the phrase "gut level" popped up in the midst of it, students assumed that the speaker must be talking of something real.)

Paul Tillich wrote and preached of the Ground of our Being experienced at the depths of our inner lives. Many of his disciples have taken him to be a theologian of introspection.

From Long Island to California sensitivity training and other human development groups are flourishing, attracting, among others, clergymen who are convinced that their ministries cannot be effective without such an experience.

Much of this is true, necessary, and good. But the whole world seems to be contemplating its navel! The list of examples is endless, describing man's insatiable fascination with himself. Somehow the church of Jesus Christ has been given over to the trend of discovering the inner man, dredging up whatever comes and calling it good not because it is inherently good but because it was dredged up. In so doing the church has fallen down on the job of providing leadership and guidance in a world that is spiritually and morally troubled. We may be swimming upstream to suggest that an encounter with the Other is needed. But it is a swim that needs to be undertaken.

Before jumping in, it is quite clear that we would be all wet in another sense if we suggested that God does not actually come to us through our inner nature. He does. Just as he spoke to the great men of faith described in scripture, so he does today, nudging us, sometimes clobbering us, in our intuition, our mind, our bodies. The "still small voice" is often coming from within. We need only take the time to be quiet and listen for it.

The point here is not to deny the inner voice. The point is to get over ourselves and begin to follow Jesus Christ, who walked in the pages of scripture and is alive and at work in our world today. We are not at all suggesting that people should stop listening to personal intuition and conscience. That would be a mistake. Throughout the history of the church some of the most significant theologians and some of the most influential confessions of faith have given prominent place to the role of conscience as a guide to Christian life. Even more relevant to our discussion: Suppose a person did decide to live his life denying what he feels, trying hard not to hear his inner voice when it says, "It's all right with me if you do this." What would the person be doing? He would be winning plaudits from some for admirable self-discipline and self-denial. But his ethic would be shallow. For one thing he would be consciously limiting the power of God, pretending that the inner reaches of personal life are off limits to the Lord, that if something comes from within, it therefore cannot be God. From personal experience most of us know that it can. Secondly, our subject would not be getting beyond himself. He would be burning up great amounts of energy simply keeping his discipline going, but his energy would be wasted. He would be focusing it on himself, because it is something of himself that he is trying to overcome. It would be far more responsible for him to forget himself and focus on God, wherever the Lord may be, within us or outside us. The issue is not one of where God is. It is a matter of who God is; and he is Other than us. That for now is enough.

On equally poor footing is the "hurt me" Christian who daily tries to climb up on his cross for all to see. He makes his decisions about how to act on the notion that, if it feels good, it must be wrong. He feels guilty about having a good time. For all of his seeming self-denial, he may be the most self-centered of all. After all, what standard of behavior does he have besides his own feelings? True, he does things in reverse. But it is still how he feels (bad) that determines what he will do in a given situation. "How can I exploit this moment to climb up on my cross and get in some personal wounds?"

Admittedly, these personalities have been presented in caricature. In the same way the comparison of a little five-year-old girl with modern man is a bit overdrawn. But one point jabs through. There is a growing fascination with self. That is not overdrawn. "It's all right with me, so I'll do it." That is the modern way of life.

All of this brings us to Superman. This comic-strip character is an excellent, unabashed image of much that is brewing within the wishes and dreams of our inner selves. He is all right, as far as we are concerned. Wouldn't life be a lot simpler if we had a Superman to do for us what the Man of Steel does for Jimmy Olsen? The inner man, left to itself, will produce such a self-gratifying Superman god.

In a day and age when personal feelings and desires are given so much nearly exclusive authority, we run into a strong headwind when we proclaim a message that comes from the Other. But the time has come to hand over the source of authority, for ultimate truth does not originate with you and me. It begins with God. He is more deserving of our trust than we are.

The time has come to begin asking a new question. We have asked long enough, "What does man need? What do the people want?" It is time for us to face the more central question in our churches and in our personal lives: "What does the Lord require?"

6

The Vague Vogue
and the Mental Mess

A group of teen-agers got up recently to give testimonies about how they had met the Lord and what he was doing in their lives. It was obvious from their presentation that they were onto something they found wonderful. Their new perspective gave them the freedom to speak out unafraid, even in front of a church full of people, most of whom were adults and complete strangers. The testimonies were spontaneous. For some reason most of the kids thought it very important to share that fact: "I really haven't prepared anything." . . . "I don't know what I am going to say, except that God will lead me." The outline of the speeches followed each speaker's train of consciousness. Personal experience was described in some detail, each one talking of how it felt and what it meant to him. No matter that speaker number three seemed to be saying the exact opposite of speaker number one. What was important was that from different personalities and backgrounds the young people felt that they were addressing the same subject.

At the rear of the sanctuary, two clergymen stood editorializing on what was taking place. One cleric leaned over to his friend and in a stage whisper announced, "They have no theology. It's all superficial gibberish, as though they were on a high, or just talking because they think Jesus is 'in.' These kids feel that if they gush emotion about Jesus, anything goes. Do you hear the way they contradict each other and don't even notice?"

It would be unfair and unwise to size up the motives of either the youth or the clergy. Suffice it to say that, throughout the history of the church, whenever there has been a spiritual awakening of any sort, there is to be seen an equal and sometimes opposite reaction on the part of those who want to preserve theological precision. The spiritualists accuse the theologians of having a dry and lifeless faith that does not excite or change personal lives. The theologians accuse the spiritualists of being so overly enthusiastic in their vague emotionalism they fail to find Christianity and to encounter the great truths of the church.

A solution to this dilemma may be found in a well-known passage of scripture that is often read as the call to worship. "The hour cometh, and now is, when the true worshippers shall worship the Father in spirit and in truth (John 4:23, KJV)." It is important to note that the words are not "in spirit *or* in truth" but "in spirit *and* in truth." Like so many other tensions within Christendom, people are tempted to settle the problem by opting for one or the other extreme.

What is so easily overlooked in our religious experience is that both God's Spirit and his eternal truth come to us from beyond ourselves. They originate in him. There is a difference between the Spirit of the living God and our emotions. While his Spirit invades our emotions and is real there, our feelings are not necessarily God. At the same time God's truth is always a step beyond us. We see through a glass darkly. It is presumptuous for us to assume that our thoughts and our experience are always right. The most arrogant thing we can do is assume that by our own figuring we can come to a knowledge of God. As men stretch to express God, there will be contradictions. The reformer Martin Luther, a man of profound openness to God, was often accused of contradicting himself. It happens.

At the time of this writing, *Jesus Christ Superstar* is a very popular rock opera, giving its version of the life of Jesus. After a successful tour, the show is now on the Great White Way in New York City. Quite a rhubarb has arisen over this production. The battle rages on the question, "Is it turning people on to Jesus, or is it just turning them on?" There can be little doubt that because of Superstar thousands of people, particularly teen-agers, have become interested in this man Jesus and have sought to learn more about him by reading the New Testament. The defense rests its case on that alone, and it is a good point.

The prosecution, however, presses on, claiming that Superstar is presenting a false picture of Jesus. Admittedly the authors of the opera, Andrew Webber and Tom Rice, had a controversial theological intention in mind. They wanted to present Jesus as a fully human being. As one of the characters sings, "He's just a man." For two thousand years people have had a hard time grasping the notion that God would fully, totally become a man. Many in the church see Jesus as a kind of Superman, "Strange visitor from another planet with powers and abilities far beyond those of mortal men," who, disguised as Jesus of Nazareth, was really not a man at all but remained God himself. This kind of heresy is called Docetism. Webber and Rice were trying to overcome it.

Unfortunately they twisted the Bible to make their point. They used scripture to provide characters and background materials, reading into scripture, failing to let scripture use them. Judas, for example, emerges as the Jack Anderson of the disciples, able to sort out the true secret about Jesus and report it to the audience. Mary Magdalen is a composite of many Marys in the New Testament, with a touch of Hollywood thrown in. As a way of enhancing the image of Jesus the man, a hint of romance between him and Mary is added to the plot. What of Jesus himself? How do we square his being just a man with the thrust of the Gospels? In *Superstar* the audience is not sure if the plot is about the man from Nazareth or the Man of La Mancha. Jesus comes off as a kind of Don Quixote, a deluded champion of goodness, taking on the windmills of life, being mocked by authorities, yet loved by those he helped. When he dies, there is no resurrection, though in the libretto accompanying the record album the resurrection passages are mentioned. In the theater heavenly music accompanies a light show, symbolizing resurrection or whatever the audience wishes. But our hero, our poor deranged hero, is dead as far as the action is concerned. Such is the bizarre by-product of reading into scripture, of using scripture rather than being guided by it.

Screams of protest arise from many corners when *Superstar* is criticized in this way. "So what if it makes a few mistakes? We do not care. All that matters is that people are reading their Bibles again."

Not quite. Without wanting to stop people from opening their Bibles, let us hasten to add that it is very easy to bring to the reading of anything, including scripture, our own preconceptions. In fact, one of the great stumbling blocks to Bible study is the very easy way in which we can use the Bible to justify whatever we want. Adolescents, frustrated by their parents, their teachers, their church, see Jesus as a great rebel against the Establishment. They delight in such stories as the prodigal son (Luke 15:11–32), feeling that they too must take off into the far country to find themselves and then be welcomed back a better person for it. At the same time, more conservative parents pick up the same Bible and find such passages sticking in their minds as "Think not that I have come to abolish the law and the prophets; I have come not to abolish them but to fulfil them (Matt. 5:17)." or "If you love me, you will keep my commandments (John 14:15)." Activists read of Jesus feeding the hungry. Pietists read of heavenly places: "In my Father's house are many rooms (John 14:2)." And let us not forget the aristocrat who wants no responsibility for the so-called riffraff. He reads Jesus' words, "For you always have the poor with you (Matt. 26:11)." Why fight Jesus? Let's leave them poor.

Are we really doing our young people a favor sending them to their Bibles to learn more of the *Superstar,* when the Bible is distinctly trying to say that Jesus is a savior? We cannot be content to let our preference for vague thinking permit us to turn to scripture to justify this or that claim or to discover more support for this or that misconception. There is only one way to come before scripture. That is prayerfully to get beyond ourselves and begin to listen.

Knowing that we have limitations on our ability to comprehend God, and caught in a time that seems to glory in confusion about the meaning of faith, we must now open the Bible and begin to encounter what the Word is saying to us.

7

The Word and the Wish

Jesus had a problem. His disciples did not seem to grasp what he was trying to say to them. It was as though they were on a different wavelength. Jesus would perform a miracle or make an important statement. The disciples would show amazement or nod agreement and then go on to ignore completely what Jesus had just done or said. Jesus might be teaching about the meek inheriting the earth, and the disciples would be squabbling over who should be first in the kingdom of Heaven. The problem of misunderstanding was so much a part of Jesus' life that John wrote his Gospel with a built-in technique to take advantage of it. Jesus makes a statement (such as telling Nicodemus that he must be born again), the listener completely misunderstands (as when Nicodemus becomes sarcastic, asking if he is to reenter his mother's womb), and then Jesus explains in more detail (telling Nicodemus more of what rebirth in the spirit really means). This is the pattern that John uses to help his reader to understand.

No matter how powerful Jesus' speaking was, he

ran into stiff opposition when his message was not what people wanted to hear. They had their own preconceptions of what a messiah was to be. The international situation colored popular thinking, in those days as in ours. The Jews were living under the thumb of Roman domination. It hurt their national pride to be a captive people. They dreamed of the day a mighty warrior would come to fight a never-ending battle for truth, justice, and the Israelite way. Such a superman was to be the Messiah, or the Christ, as they called him. When Jesus of Nazareth began his ministry and showed the power of God at work in his life, healing, walking on water, changing water into wine, the people, of course, assumed that this was their man. The Deliverer had arrived.

In Mark's narrative, chapter 8, Jesus asks his disciples who they think he is. Peter pipes up with the famous announcement, "You are the Christ (v. 29)." Okay. That sounds right to Christian ears. But there is mixed reaction as to what Jesus thought of it. Even on this occasion he does not congratulate Peter for saying the right thing. (In Matthew's account [16:16], Peter adds "the Son of the living God" to his confession, and Jesus responds most favorably. When the word "Christ" alone is mentioned, Jesus is not so warm.) Instead Jesus begins to tell the disciples not to say that sort of thing in public. He starts immediately to explain that the Son of Man must suffer many things, and be killed, and rise from the dead. Hold it! says Peter. I just got through saying you were the Christ. What is all this business about suffering and dying? You are our hero. You can't up and die on us. Knowing the devil is taking a swipe at him in Peter's words, Jesus replies, utterly disgusted, "Get behind me, Satan (Mark 8:33)."

One would have thought the resurrection should have cleared up all these problems. Certainly in many ways it did. But in Acts 1:6 we read that even as late as the day of his ascension into heaven Jesus still faces the same old thing. "When they [the apostles] had come together [with Jesus], they asked him, 'Lord, will you at this time restore the kingdom to Israel?' " Jesus had tried to bring them a new message on a new wavelength. But their sets did not pick up his channel. He offered a great hope, but they asked only of their old problems. He was God's Word made flesh, but they were ready only for the fulfillment of their own wishes.

It is a constant battle for Jesus, even today.

Perhaps in using something as commonplace as a comic strip we will get a closer look at our wishes, our preconceptions, that keep us, like the disciples, from hearing what Jesus is saying. In the rest of this book are a series of exercises, meant to be only part of a much longer process, to free us from ourselves and prepare us to receive what our God in Jesus is trying to say.

Part Two

8
The Fine Art
of Never Changing

You can always count on the staff at the *Daily Planet*. At the beginning and even at the end of every episode, they are exactly the same. Their personalities never change. Jimmy Olsen is impetuous, naïve, blundering. Lois Lane is motherly in her attitude toward Jimmy and even tries to mother Clark Kent from time to time. Perry White can be counted on to be gruff, dogmatic, and at least half a pace out of step with whatever happens to be going on around him. None of the members of this trio seems able to learn a single lesson from their many narrow escapes. No matter how much time they all spend with Superman, he has no impact on their personal lives.

Obviously this enhances the marketability of the Superman series. A certain predictability assists the audience in becoming more fully involved in each episode by feeling they know these characters. The near-ritual of Jimmy, Lois, and Perry being overwhelmed by something they stupidly assume they can handle is an essential ingredient in the story. Because it has happened so often before, the audience can confidently think to itself, There they go again; I knew they would get into trouble. It resembles the magic way hit records become popular as kids learn to hum the tune or sing the words; the same thing over and over always works.

Something would be lost if the characters changed. The audience would be confused. It would be as though three strangers were now working with Clark Kent. What if Lois could suddenly fend for herself and get out of tight jams? What if Jimmy went out after a story, got it, and brought desperate criminals to justice in the process? The plot would be nonsense. The characters have to stay inept for the sake of the series.

Beneath these considerations, however, may lie the truer motive. It is simply not the purpose of a projected hero to alter the underlying personality of the one whose imagination has projected him. The hero is to execute the wishes of a personality whose nature is already formed. Superman gets people out of predicaments. He rescues them from places they do not wish to be. He never tries to bring about any sort of reordering in the lives of the persons with whom Clark Kent must associate from day to day. Personality sameness is an important part of the continuing episodes, because personality sameness is something of value deep in human nature. We tend to be suspicious of people who change, and at deep levels we resist it within ourselves.

This is not to suggest that all types of change are against human nature. Far from it. Little boys dream of being bigger and stronger, able to play on professional athletic teams. Little girls dream of being more attractive, sexy if you will, able to catch the eye of the little boys. Whether we believe that these dreams are genuine or the products of socially taught roles, the fact remains that boys and girls spend millions of dollars annually on programs and products designed to help them change. Grown-ups are the same way. "Take Bufferin to get rid of the headache." "Buy a new car to acquire more status." "Take Geritol in the morning to be in control of your life." The whole advertising game is based on the assumption that people want to be changed in some way and will spend their money on any product that promises to bring about the type of change they want.

There is the point. It has to be the type of change the customer wants—or is told that he wants. Advertising does not tamper with that fundamental level at which values and desires lie. "You will be all of the things you want to be if you buy our product." "Our product will help you execute your desires regarding yourself." "You want fresher breath? We have just the thing for you." "Do you find that you have too much excess stomach acid? We have just what you need."

The kinds of changes that people envision for their lives are really not changes in their basic motivation. Rather they are changes in the success with which their motives are actualized. Suppose I want to be well liked. I do not want to stop wanting to be well liked. I want to change in such a way that I am better liked.

Projections come out of the deepest level of our lives, sometimes even a subconscious corner, in which we want, desire, and dream. Projections are servants of our wants, not lord of them. Naturally no projected hero is going to shake us up on this most important level of our lives. The sameness of Jimmy, Lois, and Perry, then, is a symbol of how basic human nature wants to live unaltered.

Unfortunately, there are many who turn to the church, and what they call the Christian faith (we call it pop religion), to offer only superficial change. What they really want and expect is a fulfillment of their own primitive desires.

Dietrich Bonhoeffer, in one of his early writings entitled *The Cost of Discipleship*, describes the biblical account of three men who approached Jesus ready to volunteer to become his disciples. In each case our Lord sent the man away in rather rude terms. A reading of the New Testament shows that those who eagerly sought discipleship came off rather poorly. Jesus knew that they had no inkling of what true discipleship was all about, and he refused to cater to their projected wish-filled notions. Bonhoeffer puts it this way: "No man can choose such a life for himself. No man can call himself to such a destiny, says Jesus, and his word stays unanswered. The gulf between a voluntary offer to follow and genuine discipleship is clear." Discipleship to Jesus Christ cannot come out of our concepts, but out of his.

So it is that much of our religious experience either blesses our conceptions of what ought to be or finds some way to keep the life-changing power of God from us. A few years ago the Christian education committee of a congregation is reported to have been wrestling with the basic question, "What is the meaning and purpose of Christian education?" They agreed that it was primarily for children and young people (thus they, the adults, could remain immune) and that its most important function was to train children how to live decent, moral lives, with good manners. Further discussion revealed that they were really talking about rearing children into the present life-style of their adult community. This is not the place to comment upon that educational goal—except to say that with all the social changes in our country we are always educating children for life in a world that no longer exists by the time we graduate them. More important is the fact that this particular committee meeting took place during the era when campus riots were commonplace in the headlines. People were afraid that children were getting hopelessly out of line. "We want more decency and order. Therefore, the church of Jesus Christ will provide for us decency and order." Odd that the committee members did not speak of freeing the children to become disciples of Jesus Christ. Rather they seemed suspicious of that, sensing that it might touch the children at a profound point in their lives, alter their values, and thereby threaten the whole social ball of wax. Far better to keep them under the thumb in the name of religion.

Genuine encounter with Jesus Christ is a meeting with the Other. Whenever we meet another honestly we lose a bit of control. We find that we might be changed by that relationship. The committee played it safe. They opted for blessing the status quo and training children into it.

The other strategy of pop religion is to keep the life-changing power of God from us. We observe in the Superman series the clever way our projected hero stays remote, hidden behind the spectacles of Clark Kent, always entering people's lives from the beyond. This protects the other characters from intimacy with the Man of Steel. It is intimacy that brings about personal change.

The classic example of such practice in church is what we might call "remote religion." The language of the prayers, hymns, and even the sermons can have a completely unintelligible ring. The minister himself is thought to be on a pedestal, somehow different from ordinary folk. Much has been written about this technique, and I wish I had a dollar for every time I have heard it called "irrelevant." Irrelevant it probably is. But presently in our churches we are finding stronger barriers erected against God in other ways.

A layman in a church encounters the Spirit of Christ through any number of means—in church, in private prayer groups, or just in personal prayer. He wants to share his great joy with others in his church and with the minister. What happens? All too often he is given the cold shoulder. "Let's not get fanatical about all of this." When he comes to the very place he expects to find support for his growth in the spirit, he is turned off. The church has an effective apparatus for squelching Christians who take their faith too seriously. What an insidious way to keep God from our lives! Take his name, offer his word in small doses, but never get carried away.

In defense of the church, and I consider myself a

churchman, it must be said that the old institution is growing. For all its weaknesses, it is the church that probably in one way or another started all these new converts on their way to Christ. Ministers and laymen are becoming increasingly open to experiences of the Spirit.

At the same time it is the responsibility of the church to keep people from hiding from God by using the religion of "overgush." Pouring out all kinds of feelings in the name of the Spirit may be an excellent way of keeping God at arm's length while reaping all the benefits of feeling "holier than thou." Someone recently made an amateur study of the phenomenon of talking in tongues. People get carried away with the spirit and begin to babble, as did the New Testament church. Sometimes there is an interpreter who explains the message coming through. The study revealed that in almost every case the interpreter gave a reading that was 100 percent what he already believed. Usually it was the ax he happened to be grinding at the moment. So-called experiences of the Spirit may or may not have anything at all to do with a real encounter of the Other. Very often they do not. They are just one more alternative to the real thing. People today seem drawn to Christ but unable really to encounter him. The reason is not a matter of the spirit. It is a matter of morals. We are at home in our present life-style. Even if we don't particularly like it, at least there is comfort in being familiar with it. It is extremely threatening to realize that something might change the way we live. Jesus Christ does just that. He has an ability to enter personal lives, not as a servant but as the Lord who can make all things new. Christians live a new kind of life because their wants are different.

A strong case can be made for the idea that "we are what we want." The identity of a person is quite bound up in what he wants, the things he dreams of having and becoming. Any three teen-agers may be quite different in personality. If one of them wants to go to a top-notch college, another may want to woo attractive teen-age girls and the third simply to get away from his parents. Their basic goals will have a tremendous impact on the way in which they live their lives. Sometimes these goals even take on the character of being a kind of god for them. The apostle Paul must have known how strong our wants are when he commented that we have to die to our old self when we accept Jesus Christ. We try to keep our God far from us because we do not want to die in that sense. We will cling tenaciously to our wants. Why not? They are what our life is all about, at least as far as we know it.

There are moments in life when a choice must be made. The world around us, reflected in advertising, is one way for us to go. There are few places we can turn and not be bombarded by ads. The message is the same: "You want to get to point X (by looking better, feeling better, living better) and we provide the means to get there." The way our life is to go is completely in our own hands. We chart our own future and then set out after it, aided by the products of our society.

The Bible offers another way. Biblical faith is seen

YOU'LL COVER IT?

I--I'D LIKE TO BECOME A REAL REPORTER-- LIKE CLARK KENT, AND IF YOU'D ONLY GIVE ME A CHANCE...

HMM...YOU'D PROBABLY DO A BETTER JOB THAN CLARK, AT THAT. TELL YOU WHAT I'LL DO, KID. COME BACK AGAIN IN FIVE OR TEN YEARS.....AND I MAY GIVE YOU A BREAK....

T-TEN YEARS? --THAT'S A LONG TIME!

CLARK AND LOIS RETURN TO THE NEWSPAPER OFFICE....

SO HERE YOU ARE! WHERE HAVE YOU TWO BEEN?

OUT LOOKING FOR MATERIAL --BUT NOT A THING IS STIRRING!

NOTHING, EH? GET DOWN TO THE GAYFORD MANSION! -- THOMAS GAYFORD HAS BEEN SLAIN BY A MYSTERIOUS PERSON NAMED "THE ARCHER". HE REFUSED TO PAY THE AMOUNT DEMANDED!

WHAT --?!

"THE ARCHER"! SOUNDS MELO- DRAMATIC!

--AND EXCITING

YOU, EH? IT DOESN'T TAKE YOU LONG TO SHOW UP WHEREVER NEWS IS BEING MADE!

THAT'S OUR BUSINESS!

HAVE YOU ANY IDEA WHO THIS "ARCHER" MAY BE, CASEY?

NONE AT ALL--YET, BUT WE HAVE SOME INTERESTING CLUES.

WHY DON'T YOU COOK UP A NEW COME-BACK?

THAT ONE'S A LITTLE SHOP- WORN!

QUIET, YOU TWO-- OR I'LL HAVE YOU RUN OFF THE PLACE!

3

© 1941 Superman, Inc. Renewed 1969 by National Periodical Publications, Inc.

in a man like Abraham. How different he was from the man who watches commercials telling him how he can be all of the things he wants to be. How different from the man who sets his personal goals and then lets nothing distract him on his quest for them. Abraham heard the voice of God telling him to follow God wherever the Lord might lead. "Who knows what the future holds? Follow me." Abraham did.

Isn't that the call to discipleship? Jesus made use of the phrase "follow me" in gathering his disciples. After Peter had made his confession, "You are the Christ," Jesus corrected him by telling how the son of man must suffer many things. Then Jesus told his disciples to take up their crosses and follow him. He did not really spell out exactly what that meant, and no doubt the disciples were somewhat stumped by it. "Follow me (Mark 8:34)" is all he said. In John's account, after the resurrection the disciples were on a beach with Jesus, and he three times asked Peter if he loved him. Then simply, "Follow me (John 21:19)," he said.

Life is different. It is new, when we obey that call. To many it will seem that we are misguided, and even maladjusted. How much our society worships those who are in control of their own futures! It is a life of trust, following Jesus. I cannot tell you where it will lead. I can say that life as it is now known will pass away. There is more adventure. Yet there is more calm. Something completely new and wonderful will begin when we trust him with the most important part of our lives—the future.

9

You and Me, God

There is a not-so-subtle aspect to the job description of our beloved Kryptonian. It is not mentioned as publicly as, say, his fight for justice, but then many episodes really do not deal with the judicial process at all.

Superman seems, in fact, to have another primary reason for being: the health, wealth, and happiness of certain persons, sometimes at the expense of others. Most particularly he works to help Jimmy Olsen, Lois Lane, and Perry White. To his credit we need bear in mind that the reporters are usually the innocent victims of the shenanigans of the bad guys.

Now obviously if a youngster is going to go and dream up a hero, he is not going to be dumb enough to give that hero the freedom to turn on him. Who could ever imagine a genie coming out of a magic lantern and refusing to go along with the wishes of the lad who rubbed the lamp? So it is with Superman. He is not going to go against the best interests of the select group with whom the audience identifies. The ten-year-old munching popcorn in the first row of the movie house Saturday afternoon sees Jimmy tied up in an abandoned mine shack as the fuse on the dynamite gets shorter and shorter. His impulse is empathetic; he sides with Jimmy. "Come on, Superman, get my friend out of here." In some cases the plea from the audience may even be "Come on, Superman, get *us* out of here." Needless to say, time after time, the *whoosh* of wind is heard as Superman arrives right on cue.

He is thought to be the defender of "our" kind of people, "our" way of life—us. Some of the more recent episodes have dropped "American way" from the introduction. Still the impression lasts. It is inconceivable that the Man of Steel would side with Moscow, or Peking, or Hanoi. He is a white, healthy American of Anglo-Saxon appearance. One wonders how a strange visitor from another planet could so easily become so provincial. He never associates with the bad guys except to trick them into giving themselves away. He never transgresses the rules of decency, though some speculate that Lois Lane wishes he would. He is, in short, a goody-goody, according to the middle-class, middle-aged, white American definition.

That such a character has points in common with God in the public eye, or with what a godly life is to be, is a point that has been overworked. It has been popular in recent years to expose the narrowmindedness of the "God-is-on-our-side" brand of religion and patriotism. In many cases it has been overdone, and a bit naïvely, by writers who have little more to say than "Look at all the hypocrites in church." Unfortunately these writers have not been at a loss for data to fill their paragraphs and round out their essays. We white American men have assumed that God is a white man. Our black brothers are now saying, "We think he's black." Our sisters in the liberation movement say, "Who cares what color she is?" God is taking on the image of the believer. (Dare we say, the image of the projector?)

A discussion leader in a college group a few years ago remarked that if an athlete prayed for victory before a contest, and if his faith were genuine, he would win that contest. Someone in the group asked what would happen if his opponent, also a devout Christian, also prayed to win that same contest? Stunned silence. It had never occurred to the discussion leader that his opponent might also be a faithful man and pray for his defeat. "God is on my side. He looks like me, does what I want. He is one of my crowd." Finally a witty member of the group relieved the embarrassment by suggesting that in his infinite wisdom God would make it rain that day.

Before we toss any more stones at these already too battered souls, let us take a deep breath and ask what is really going on. In recent years the opinion makers in church, the men who write the books, teach in seminaries, and are on the speaking circuit, have made hay by setting up straw men they could then knock down. "God is on our side" is the name for a kind of belief that has come under tremendous attack within the church. The opinion makers have knocked the patriots who believe that God may have some American blood in his heavenly veins. They have knocked the pietists who have the audacity to ask God for things in prayer and assume that they will receive them. They have knocked the white, the suburban, the adult, the male. All this has taken place with some good reason and justification. But any indictment that is not also self-indictment is judging, and it assumes "I will not be judged." It is presuming "I am without guilt, so I can throw the first stone." It is a sham.

What has happened? A reverse "God-is-on-our-side" theology has grown up. God is thought to be on the side of those who knock down the straw man. Jesus was a rebel. Jesus had long hair. The critics become guilty of the same sin they saw in those they criticized. They thought God was exclusively their man. He was on their side. "God is on my side when I knock the people who believe God is on their side."

I believe that we are ready to move beyond that absurdity, that we are able to look at what scripture teaches rather than switch arrogantly and spitefully from one pet project to another. Paul writes to the church at Rome (Romans 8:28,31), "We know that in everything God works for good with those who love him, who are called according to his purpose. . . . What then shall we say to this? If God is for us, who is against us?" God is for us. He is on our side in the battle of life. Why not stand up and say it? In Christ he has given us the power to overcome the obstacles that are put in our path.

The book by Brother Andrew, *God's Smuggler,* is great reading. It is the story of how the author smuggled Bibles behind the Iron Curtain to Christians often deprived of an opportunity to read or to hear God's word. The story is exciting. Andrew repeatedly is about to run out of money, out of gas, out of Bibles, out of ways to get past the guards. Time after time God intervenes to provide the way. One is struck by the great truth that Brother Andrew radically trusts his God. He has given his life radically to God's service. At the time the book was written God had already shown that he was on Andrew's side because Andrew was doing God's will.

This example is not unique. Rather it is but one of many illustrations pointing to the truth that our God is willing to intervene in this life on behalf of his people, on behalf of those who have given their lives to him. God has already intervened on behalf of us all in Jesus Christ.

Here are a few guidelines as we ponder how to be creative and responsible in our living out the fact that God is on our side.

(1) It begins with the personal. Jesus lived and died for me. How often today laymen stand up to give their testimonies, saying, "For a long time I knew about Jesus. I heard the preacher describe him. I thought I believed in him. But now I know that he really means something to me." It is that kind of faith, realizing that God has come to you and to me in a personal way, that gets us started.

(2) Our faith becomes corporate. We need the fellowship of other Christians. Many people are finding that the large cathedral-style architecture of church sanctuaries is not conducive to spiritual growth because it denies them access to other Christians. The preaching of the word is vital, as are the sacraments, and these usually take place in sanctuaries. Who can

deny what can happen when Billy Graham preaches to thousands of listeners? But it is in discussion rooms, in living rooms, that many breakthroughs in faith are now so often occurring. One man began with a prayer service on Friday evenings with eight or ten people attending. He has since removed a wall to expand his living room and accommodate the crowd that is yet able to maintain a personal fellowship.

The faith that is growing out of these small groups bears a witness that is profound. People say that their lives have been changed—and so has their relation to their local church. One might think the living room would become an alternative to the established church. But this is not happening. The church offers something needed. No matter how much Jesus did with his small group of disciples, it was his habit to be regular in his attendance at regular services of worship. Apparently even he was able to draw from it. Some people who had been dissatisfied with their local church are coming back after experiences in living rooms. They come back to continue growth. They come back wanting others in their church to share the joy they now have in their lives. Jesus Christ left his small group a commission to go out to others. Our local churches are not to be abandoned by those who have found a deeper faith. Rather our local churches are the first responsibility, the first place to share in love what we have found.

(3) Our faith is not exclusive. God so loved the *world*. The invitation is to all. "You shall be my witnesses in Jerusalem and in all Judea and Samaria and to the end of the earth (Acts 1:8)." The book of Acts

has, as a constant theme, the expansion of the gospel ethnically, geographically, nationally until the day all men hear it. God is on the side of those who have given their lives to him, using these people as his ambassadors to all men. God is only on our side to the extent that we are reaching out, because God's work is outreaching work.

(4) Therefore, God is on our side in a purposeful way. It is not enough to fill up our cup and let it run over. We need to share it. The notion that God is on our side is not a static fact on which to build our status. It is a dynamic fact coming to reality as we act, as we fulfill his purposes for us.

The record of modern church history is that when we in the family of God are afraid to live the faith that God is "on our side" in his love, we shrivel. We become chronic complainers about what others are or are not doing to be relevant. Our missions overseas begin to collapse, and in spite of ourselves we become provincial and narrow—we see no point to starting new churches. When we cannot say "God is for us," what message have we to offer?

It is when we know God's love for us that we reach out and fulfill our mission. No man has ever encountered Jesus Christ who did not want to share Christ with others. Projected heroes such as Superman may be on our side for our own sake. God is on our side for the sake of others.

10

Who Me? You've Got to Be Kidding, Lord!

After a few years, the many distinct stories of Superman's heroics begin to merge into one. The reporters have got themselves into an incredible crisis. The dynamite is about to blow. The crooks are about to shoot them. The log to which they are tied is about to slide into the saw. The monster is about to find them and eat them alive.

Suddenly a *whoosh* of wind, perhaps even some flying debris if the entrance happens to be through a wall (no one is hit by the debris, of course), and Superman arrives. Immediately he attacks the problem —throwing the dynamite thousands of feet into the sky where it explodes (harmlessly), distracting the crooks who fire at him only to have their bullets bounce off his chest, braking the saw, corralling the monster.

The plot is brought to a happy ending because Superman acts completely on his own to set things straight. He does not bring the police with him, although they may later appear on the scene to look after the business of arresting any already captured outlaws. Superman makes no effort at all to bring Jimmy, Lois, or Perry into the process of solving the problem. If they are tied up, he leaves them tied up until everything is under control. Mortals have no role to play in the work of Superman.

This is a not uncommon characteristic of projected magic heroes. In the TV series *I Dream of Jeannie*, the heroine grants wishes, does good deeds, even pulls a prank or two by folding her arms and bobbing her head. Never does she perform a miracle by asking others to share the process with her. One could not imagine the genie in a magic lantern granting three wishes by consulting his master—"Let's cooperate on this thing." Projected heroes work alone.

It is simpler that way, more direct. The return of characters like Superman in this particular time in our culture's history may be due in part to our growing frustration with collective processes and a genuine craving for monarchy or enlightened despotism. Why else when life seems bad in this country do protesters blame the President and so constantly demand that he turn things around? They must wish he were a beneficent dictator. It is a time when people want to cut red tape, get things done, do what they want without having to file endless applications, forms, and order blanks and then on top of that have to wait for the powers to grind out an "okay" or "not okay" for them to do what they wish. Little wonder, as this page is being written, that the book and the movie *The Godfather* are smash hits in our society. No matter what we think of violence and crime, Americans seem to crave the directness, the power, and the dispatch with which the Godfather can get his work done. It would be nonsensical to dream up a hero who was a bureaucrat working through channels. Give us a hero with sovereignty to do what we want him to do.

Another rationale for Superman's working alone is seen when we ask, "What is the alternative?" When the chips are down do we seriously think an intelligent Kryptonian is going to trust Jimmy Olsen? And to collaborate with the bad guys is out of the question. He has to work alone.

A very dim view of human nature and human capacity is revealed in all this. Every earthling is by nature either a bumbling buffoon, by circumstance at his level of incompetence, or by every social standard bad. Only the strange visitor from another planet is good and able.

We should expect this phenomenon. When we were kids and dreamed up our heroes to do battle for us, why did we do it? In fact, why in more adult ways do we do it today? Very often it is because we feel ourselves to be incapable of getting through to others or of bringing about the ends we want. At the same time we feel that others are misguided, lacking in understanding. There is a hint of "I'll get you, world" in the dreams of people who project. It is the kind of escapism that grows often out of uncertainty, frustration, and what one modern author calls an "I'm not okay" position. Really, there seem few other reasons for us to dream up these projections.

The end result is a fantasized character entirely different from man as we see man to be. There is no common ground on which our hero and our peers or ourselves could cooperate. If such ground were found it would call into question the very need for having projected our hero in the first place.

Some might ask, "Don't we have here at last the perfect comparison with God?" It certainly looks that way. There were the disciples quaking in their sandals out in a boat, tossing and turning on a stormy sea. Jesus, wake up! Help! We're going to drown! Jesus without the help of any disciples calmed the sea.

Then there was the time at a wedding when they ran out of wine. Everybody was just high enough that more wine was demanded, not quite high enough to want to stop drinking. Jesus did it again. Presto! The water became wine.

Let there be no mistaking it, God is very much able to do things without relying on man. Praise the Lord for that. He created the universe without human assistance. He created human life, though happily he lets us help in the process of propagating the species. Again, praise the Lord! Most importantly the work of our salvation is his doing in Jesus Christ. We would be in sad straits if our ultimate destiny rested with our own efforts.

I once heard a preacher offer a saying told him by still another preacher. "Every church must have something in it that only God can do." In our hustle and bustle, moving from planning committee to task force to fund drive, we rightfully try to do our best for God. But we keep the church life so busy with our doing, what do we expect him to do in our church? Most meetings wind up deciding which members will carry out what action. How many meetings end with a prayer offering a part of the work to God and trusting him to carry through?

Great things are taking place today both in the social action realm and in the more pietistic spiritual realm, because people are putting their trust in God to lead them. Supplies are arriving in the nick of time. Desperately needed money is turning up. Lives are being changed. All this is happening because men and women are saying, "God, I need your help. I hold before you my problem and ask your help." They are not asking selfishly or in vain. They are asking in trust, and God is replying. That kind of faith has the courage to tackle tasks most institutions are afraid to touch. That kind of faith gets things done.

Our God can do on his own everything any projected hero can do. *He can also do more.* He can elect to act with people and through people. He can use people, inspire people, lead people. It has been said that in most cases when God wants to get something done he begins by choosing a man, calling him, working through him. Abraham, Moses, Elijah, Paul, Martin Luther, Martin Luther King—the spirit of God has moved in these lives, and history has been made.

This is where the biblical message encounters us in a way foreign to our national inclinations. When it comes to doing "God's work" people run for the exits. "How could God act through me? Why would he need to?"

Remember Moses? We think of him as a man of tremendous faith, one of those characters who fall from the sky, as if by magic, ready from birth to do God's work. But this was not the case. One day, long after he had fled from Egypt to save his hide, Moses was tending the flock of his father-in-law on the side of a mountain. God came to Moses that day in a burning bush and found it most difficult to get his message through. Moses, it seems, had too many preconceived notions about how God did his business. When the Lord said, "I have seen the affliction of my people who are in Egypt, and have heard their cry because of their taskmasters; I know their sufferings, and I have come down to deliver them out of the hand of the Egyptians, and to bring them up out of that land (Exod. 3:7–8)," Moses undoubtedly thought God had a pretty good idea; more power to you, Lord. But then God's words took Moses by surprise. "Come, I will send you to Pharaoh that you may bring forth my people (Exod. 3:10)."

It was more than Moses could comprehend. If God intended to bring the Israelites out of Egypt, why didn't he do it himself? He was God, wasn't he? "Who am I that I should go to Pharaoh?" asked Moses. It seemed utterly incredible. Besides, Moses had handicaps. He stuttered. What was God doing?

The tendency to believe that if God is God he will do everything himself is a factor so basic to human nature that even a great leader like Moses was influenced by it, that is, until he encountered the living God.

Encounter with God leaves us ever awake to two great truths. God is able to do miraculous things for us when we trust him. At the same time, God often chooses to perform his wonders by working through human beings, even through our modern-day Moseses who cannot believe Almighty God would ever single them out to do his work. His greatest help comes to us when we set about the work of actually doing his will.

11

Over and Over Again

When my son was three years old, it occurred to me that my wife and I had developed, as a technique for putting him to bed, something of a liturgy. Certain words were said. I carried him about his room, saying particular things to him. The door was left at a certain angle, or at least he was given the impression that the angle was the same. The process was repeated religiously every night. If I left something out, or let slip the wrong phrases, he corrected me and seemed less able to get himself to sleep.

Realizing what was occurring, we worked to free him of this process. But it was most interesting to speculate about what was happening and to wonder if perhaps we had before us a parable of human nature. I think we did. Alvin Toffler in his book *Future Shock* writes of how people living in a world of rapid change need to cling to some rituals, some parts of life that will not change. Even popular TV shows observe a certain ritual. Ushers could hand us bulletins as we take to our sofas to watch Dean Martin, or *Laugh-In*, or Johnny Carson.

The actual words vary from show to show, but the agenda or liturgy does not. Each show follows a rigorous, repetitious order. Carson, for example, does a monologue, does a bit with Ed McMahon, brings on guest one, guest two, etc. The Superman stories follow an equally rigid ritual. So it goes in our churches. We get used to worshiping our God in patterned ways that soon become routine.

The question for all Christians is: How do we keep our need for sameness from robbing our God of his freedom? God is free to change his mind. In the biblical account of the flood, we read that God was sorry he had created man and decided to hose down the creation, with the exception of the ark dwellers, and start again. Throughout scripture we read alternately of the wrath and the mercy of the Lord. At one time, God is an angry judge punishing his people. A bit later he is a loving father rewarding his people. God is free. All of us know from our own experience that he cannot be programmed by us to respond in a definite way. He comes to us and touches our lives at times, at places, and in ways only he could have anticipated.

Yet, through it all, God has a constancy. "O Thou who changest not . . ." we sing. "God is a spirit, infinite, eternal, and unchangeable," some of us learned from the catechism. Behind the seeming vacillation between wrath and mercy is the constant justice of the Lord. Behind the seemingly random ways in which God breaks into our lives is the Holy Spirit always ready, always waiting for just the right moment to invade the privacy of our inner life. This God who is free to come to us as he wills is a God whose being is constant: "thou art the same (Ps. 102:27)," said the psalmist with confidence and relief. The writer to the Hebrews echoed the notion: "Jesus Christ is the same yesterday and today and for ever (Heb. 13:8)."

Though we can be sure that God is an Other who is constant in his being and purpose, justice, and love —we must still concede that his constancy is beyond our comprehension. We always see through that glass darkly. Our words about him, our thoughts, our prayers, our expectations are less than the real thing. When we institutionalize or fossilize our concept of him, we arrive at something of a being with constancy. But that being is less than God. It is like me and the Grand Canyon. I have read about that huge chasm. I have seen pictures of it, shown me by returning tourists. But I have not yet stood on the edge of the Grand Canyon and been taken up by what I am sure must be the breathtaking awe of it. How silly I would be if I insisted that my concept of the Grand Canyon were the ultimate truth about it, that there was nothing more to understand, that my concept was unchangeable. The Grand Canyon does not really change. But this does not give me license to have an inaccurate, unchanging picture of it. I need to be willing constantly to be open to change in my awareness in order to be drawn closer to that which changes not.

This is the difference between a projection and an encounter. We project a being limited by our own concepts to a sameness defined by us. We encounter another, different from us, challenging us to grow in our understanding.

So to Superman. As was pointed out, there is sameness or constancy to the personalities of the characters in the drama. This can also be said of the plot and the role Superman plays in it. It is as though he were a computer programmed a certain way, a reflex that could not help responding in a particular fashion to particular stimuli. We do not just project heroes to pass the time of day. We project them with a job description. We want them to do definite things, and when or if they fail it is most disappointing. This is all too true of Superman and the god of pop religion.

Superman is limited to a repetitious role in that he always delivers the good guys from a precarious, painful situation and returns them to a place where they are more comfortable. Good guys are supposed to be comfy. It is the function of the deliverer to be sure that this is the way it is.

All of us seek a certain sense of comfort in life, a certain psychic and physical state of being at ease. This is natural. There is nothing wrong with it, in itself. But the warning light should come on to tell us that we are getting into trouble when we assume that comfort is supposed to be built into the order of creation, or when we are irresponsible in our concept of how comfort is to be had.

Superman offers an irresponsible deliverance from distress because he sets out only to change the environment. His work is to reinstate the familiar, same, comfortable conditions. His only task is to rid the world of whatever upsets normalcy and to get those dear people back to the office safe and sound. It is the conditions rather than individual spirit that must change.

Let there be no mistake. God sometimes acts in the same way. He parted the waters of the Red Sea; in fact, the children of Israel came to the shores of the sea because God was delivering them from intolerable conditions in Egypt. Jesus calmed a sea, provided food, made wine—all in an effort to make life a little nicer.

But there is more to what the power of God offers, something we would rarely expect an almighty champion to provide. He offers us a new relationship to our environment. The apostle Paul wrote, "I have learned, in whatever state I am, to be content (Phil. 4:11)." These are words made doubly powerful by the realization that he wrote from a dungeon. He was able to be content although in jail because in his faith he knew a higher bondage to Jesus Christ. It was this Jesus who said, "Blessed are those who mourn. . . . Blessed are the meek (Matt. 5:4–5)." There is a group therapy process for people struggling to regain and maintain emotional stability. One of the slogans the leaders put into the minds of participants to recall in times of stress is "This is merely a distressing outer environment." It is a technique to keep free and stable what is going on inside. The hidden assumption is that the real problem in life is not out there in the environment. It is inside you and me. Jesus knew this. Paul knew it: "I have learned, in whatever state I am, to be content."

Immediately there are many readers who protest. With the intolerable conditions of human life, how can so pious a sentiment as that be uttered? It sounds as though we are saying to the person in the ghetto, Stay there and be content. Jesus loves us. He'll take care of you in heaven. It sounds as though we are saying to the victims of all kinds of social injustice, If you are unhappy, straighten out your spirit and all will be well.

But such is hardly the case. Who are the people who have brought about the greatest social revolutions in history, the kinds of revolutions that have not been merely chaotic orgies leading to more repression but the revolutions that really improve man's lot? I would include Jesus in the list, of course. But also Paul for the way in which he opened doors of understanding to men of all nationalities and religious backgrounds. "I can be all things to all people in order to win some to Christ." This is an attitude far more open and revolutionary than that of many of our modern radicals or liberals. I would list Martin Luther, in self-confinement in a monastery, prayerfully uncovering truths that have triggered some of the most significant social changes in history. And his namesake, Martin Luther King, Jr., was a man willing to be beaten, to be imprisoned, finally to be murdered because, as he said, "I've been to the mountaintop . . . and I've seen the Promised Land. . . . Mine eyes have seen the glory of the coming of the Lord." He had a kind of contentment that converted any condition to the glory of God. Need it be added that he brought about social change? These people had the resources of spirit not to need worldly comfort or demand it of their Lord.

The activist challenge is rather shallow. Unless we have the faith of Paul, unless we are able to experience the kind of bondage to Christ that endures earthly hardship, we are wholly unable to do anything to help our brother in the ghetto, our brother the victim. He will see through us and send us home. It is all too easy to work for justice from the vantage point of contentment, comfort, and security. The poor are sick of that kind of help.

The One we encounter in scripture invites us to accept a faith that is free to be at home in pleasant conditions and in miserable ones, ready to be all things to all people, in order that some may be helped to a better life in faith and in body.

A word to the activist critic: Paul is not offering a pious phrase to the man in the ghetto. He is talking to you. It is not a matter of condoning social injustice; let us all be upset about that and work to stamp it out. Rather the words call on all of us not to let our faith be bound in any way by personal hardship, pain, or inconvenience. In whatsoever state *we* are, or have to be, let us be content to work there for Jesus Christ. Discipleship to Jesus Christ does not always take place under the same conditions. We never know where he may lead us.

Superman is limited to a repetitious role in that he always saves his friends from death. I recall thinking one afternoon as I sat before the great one-eyed monster known affectionately as the tube, "Lois Lane will live forever." She is a decent girl. She works for a respectable outfit. She knows Superman, and he likes her. It almost seems that he has a contract with her to make sure she survives. What a nice arrangement!

Projections are supposed to do that. They are supposed to deliver when the chips are down.

Jesus has said, "I am the resurrection and the life;

he who believes in me, though he die, yet shall he live, and whosoever lives and believes in me shall never die (John 11:25–26)." He was speaking of life eternal with God in the life after the grave. "I go to prepare a place for you [and] when I go and prepare a place for you, I will come again and will take you to myself, that where I am you may be also (John 14:2–3)."

In earthly life, however, we know that people do not live forever. They may not be around for the next episode. No matter how deep and real their faith, death awaits them. It is the facing of this death that brings us right up against our concept of God. We know him best as we see him in the context of death's inevitability. Indeed, we know our own faith in terms of what we conceive about God and the end.

Happily today there are many examples of what might be called "Faith healing." Many a prayer group has had some results from prayer that can only be called miracles. Incurable illnesses are cured. Doctors and nurses speak about their work with patients, of praying with them, and of incredible cures that stretch medical knowledge. "It was the Lord," they say. I have no doubt that it was. God often rescues us from death. He not only heals disease but he miraculously delivers people from car accidents, natural disasters, and many other events that could well have spelled the end.

But, unlike the impression we might have of Lois Lane, who I believed was programmed to live forever, everyone in real life dies. The special acts of God merely postpone death. Even Lazarus is now dead. A man cured of terminal illness will die later of something else. We need to come to grips with the twofold

nature of the God we encounter. On the one hand he
has the power to cure and sometimes he does. But on
the other hand it is his will that these cures are merely
postponements of the inevitable when we must depart
earthly life.

Perhaps the most bitter, difficult task that confronts
a Christian is to counsel a person who has just lost a
loved one. "I prayed that he would live. And he died.
There can't be a God." It is very hard work in faith to
accept a God who is not programmed continuously to
keep us alive.

Sometimes, in our faith, projected wishes have
tainted our notions of truth. We confuse magic and religion. Magic tries to manipulate fate to bring about a
desired result. Religion encounters God in the context
of "Thy will be done." Magic is always the same:
The rabbit comes out of the hat; Lois is saved. But encountering God is not quite so predictable. The happy
ending does not always come. The fight is sometimes
lost.

The first person Jesus ran into coming down the
mountain from his famous sermon was a leper who
knelt in front of him. "Lord, if you will, you can make
me clean (Matt. 8:2)." How different that is from seeing Lois tied up in a cave knowing that, of course,
Superman wants to save her; of course, he is on his
way; of course, he will do it. Our prayers to Jesus
need to be founded in trust. There is nothing he cannot
do for us. But we need also to recall the words of one
leper who encountered the person of Jesus Christ:
"Lord, if you will."

Our God is not programmed to do the same things for

us over and over. He is free. He may call us to unexpected circumstances. He will one day be present as we die. The only certainty we have is his love for us, his constant presence with us. And that is enough.

12

Get Lost

In those Saturday afternoon matinees at the movie house, one of the most exciting and predictable parts was the exit of the hero. The Lone Ranger had the best one, I thought. Having delivered the town from baddies, he mysteriously dropped out of sight.

Meanwhile, back in the sheriff's office someone would ask, "Who was that masked man? I wanted to thank him."

"You mean, you don't know? Why, he's the Lone Ranger!"

With that we would be given a hasty glimpse of the hind sides of Scout and Silver, as Tonto and the Lone Ranger rode off. "Hi-yo, Silver, away!" The William Tell Overture further multiplied the goose bumps.

The townspeople never had a chance to thank him. Come to think of it, thanking someone was not a part of the plot in any of those serials. Superman had an ability to *whoosh* away, up in the air, as quickly as he could *whoosh* down to the scene of the crisis. Having done his work he was gone.

In the making of the drama, this quick disappearance permitted him to find his clothes in the phone booth or storeroom where he left them and return to the office. There in the guise of Kent he would be razzed by the other reporters for having missed an incredible rescue by Superman. The audience would always be in on Kent's spoof. But, more important, the stage would be set for the beginning of the next episode, at which time the reporters would all be in the office. The same is true of the Lone Ranger. That series depended upon the masked man and his Indian friend happening upon adventures. Therefore, it was necessary to get them out on the road so that they could plausibly happen onto something again at the beginning of next week's show.

There is more here than staging, however. Because our projections obviously are not a reality beyond ourselves, other than ourselves, we do not carry on a relationship with them beyond the time they are needed. What would be duller than Superman hanging around the lounge of the *Daily Planet* chewing the fat with Jimmy, or the Lone Ranger staying to have supper with the sheriff and his family? Exit must follow completion of task, because task is the only reason for being.

Such a plot construction leaves out "Thank you." I recall once preaching a sermon on prayer. In this sermon I talked about six different kinds of prayer. I cannot now remember the list. But I do remember the remark made by a member of my congregation at the back door of church. "Fine sermon, except you forgot thanksgiving." After all the time I had spent on the sermon, my parishioner was right. I had omitted perhaps the most important kind of prayer there is. It is a mistake I have not repeated.

Part of the relationship that exists with our God after he has delivered us is a relationship of thanksgiving. When Jesus healed the ten lepers, only one of them returned to give him thanks. "Where are the nine? (Luke 17:17)" he asked. That is a good question. Where do people go after they have received what they want? Were they merely using Jesus in a superstitious sense? Where do families go after the baptisms, after the last teen-ager graduates from youth fellowship, after daughter is married? There are many ways in which people use the Body of Christ today and then expect it to exit from their lives when it has performed its function for them.

The challenge of Christian encounter is to stretch our needs to the other side of fulfillment and express thanksgiving. The God who meets us in what he does for us is not a God who exits flashily when his work is done. The name given Jesus by the Holy Spirit is Immanuel, which means "God with us." Jesus said to his disciples when his earthly ministry was drawing to a close, "Lo, I am with you always (Matt. 28:20)." *Faith at Work* magazine carried this quote in the April 1972 issue: "The proof of the resurrection is not in the empty tomb but in the spirit-filled fellowship." Even the act in the past has a contemporary thrust, as the one who acted is alive and present. It is the awareness of this fact that causes people in spirit-filled fellowships continually to utter two phrases: "Praise you, Jesus. Thank you, Jesus."

As we have already mentioned, people tend to project magic heroes during those moments in their lives when they are frustrated and are up against the limits of their abilities. For this reason the dream hero is expected to be present and helpful at those times when people cannot fend for themselves. There is no sense requesting a projected hero to "Give us this day our daily bread." We can do that for ourselves. Rather it is the moment of crisis that calls for the hero.

In the comic series, Superman remains incognito, cleverly disguised as a mild-mannered reporter, right up to that moment when superhuman action is required. Only then does he make his move and appear on the scene. Jimmy, Lois, and sometimes even Perry go about their business with a "Who needs Superman?" attitude, pursuing stories, having adventures, and finally getting into a predicament that renders them helpless. Then, almost prayerfully, they moan, "Oh, if Superman were only here!"

Church people call this "Foxhole Christianity." The term comes from the prayers offered by young men in our armed services who suddenly found religion in a foxhole when enemy bombs and bullets threatened to end their lives. But it has been a derogatory term. There is something unfortunate about the person who thinks of God as one might think of a tire jack. When all is well, the jack is locked up in the trunk, and the driver assumes that it will be there when needed. Under favorable conditions it is usual to keep the jack out of sight, out of mind. Many people who adamantly refuse to attend church say, "I know you are there. When I need God, I'll give you a call." For valid reasons this attitude has infuriated church people.

This, however, does not deny the validity of the

foxhole experience. It was in a terrible storm when he was afraid for his life that Martin Luther gave his life to Christ. It was on a stormy sea that John Newton gave his life to Christ, stopped his slave trading, began working for liberation, and later penned the words to the well-known hymn, "Amazing Grace." What happens to us in these moments of crisis can have a lasting effect upon the very center of our lives. It is when the alcoholic reaches his moment of crisis, knowing he needs help and seeking it, that help can be made available to him in ways that will radically change his whole life. So it is the moment of crisis that is often needed to bring us to our senses, awakening us to the need to ask help from God.

The difference between the fantasies we project and the God we encounter has little to do with what goes on in the critical moments. We dream of heroes who will deliver us. God can do the same. The difference is that the projection is limited to the boundary of our ability. The crisis past, he vanishes. But God has a lasting impact upon the way we live from that time forth. Martin Luther did not forget his moment with God when the storm was over.

There is always the feeling of superstition or luck when a dream comes true. There is the awesome realization of meeting another when God intervenes in the crisis and makes his presence felt. We cannot forget that. We know that he is real, that he acts, that he is with us. Foxhole Christianity is still Christianity. It only becomes a fraud if it ceases when the bombs stop falling.

13

Clark, Take Off Your Clothes!

Clark Kent is a nice guy. But he doesn't do anything for anybody, except in those rare moments when he simply has no time to change into Superman. He is usually a rather bland, retiring sort of chap, working the nine-to-five shift within a comfortable bureaucracy, doing his job and not making any waves. He is the kind of person a company would be glad to hire, though perhaps it might hesitate about promoting him too high up the ladder. He is what we might call the typical workingman. His life, as we know it, revolves around work. Where he lives, what kind of car he drives, whether or not he goes to church are unimportant compared to the central fact that he is a mild-mannered person, nice to have around the office.

Kent is the link to us. He is "typical." He is Dad. He is who most of us will be when we grow up.

But we really wish we could be Superman, or at least have a Superman around to work for us. It was not uncommon on the playground two and a half decades ago for my friends and me to take turns being Superman, running around as if flying to do deeds that were daring in our minds. It is food for thought whether these same wishes are not carried now far into adolescence, as we see young people in open rebellion against the Clark Kents of our society while at the same time aping some of Captain Marvel's, or Batman's, or Superman's antics, flying in their minds, aided by hallucinatory drugs. Superman is our dream-projected self.

This feeling about our nature is one so basic to human experience that the writers of the Bible incorporated it almost immediately. In the first two chapters of Genesis there are two completely different accounts of how the world began and how people were created. In the first tale, man is created in the image of God, the pinnacle of a cosmic creation. What great unfathomable possibilities we have as God's highest creative achievement! Then, as if starting all over again, the second account describes man being created from the dust of the ground like any other animal. We sense ourselves lucky to have a better lot than the dogs. It is that old feeling popularly put in the phrase "We

© 1939 Detective Comics, Inc. Renewed 1966 by National Periodical Publications, Inc.

dream of being perfect, but we are afraid we are not even average." Genesis 1 offers us the dream of being perfect, the Superman. Genesis 2 is the fear of not being even the average Clark Kent.

In the office of the *Daily Planet* the relationship between these two natures is revealed. What we find is not surprising, though perhaps a bit disappointing. The phone rings. It's Jimmy. He is at a phone booth fifty miles outside Metropolis. The baddies have captured Miss Lane, and they are coming after him. "Mr. Kent, help!" There is a sound of a scuffle, and the phone is hung up.

Using his telescopic vision, Kent looks all the way out to the spot by the road where the crooks are dragging Jimmy to their car. "This 'ooks like a job for Superman!" He dashes from behind his desk, down the hall to the door of a storeroom, with a look this way and that to make sure no one will spot him. Quickly he slips into the room. Our young eyes are spared the embarrassment of watching the mild-mannered reporter disrobe. The next sequence is Superman bounding through the window. Then we see him stretched out against the skyline of a city as he flies over it.

How much time do you suppose Clark Kent could have saved if he had cut out all that monkey business about taking off his clothes? He could have raced to the window and, necktie flapping in the breeze, gained at least a 60-second head start. When you are traveling faster than a speeding bullet that is quite a long time.

For the purpose of Superman-Kent, which, as we have already mentioned, is to serve the other employees at the *Daily Planet,* it is most convenient to perpetuate this little charade. If people knew where Superman was, he would be besieged by requests for help. Jesus himself was often so swamped by the needs of the mobs that pressed around him he had to skip meals to keep on with the work. Some interpreters even suggest that he told those whom he had helped not to tell anyone what had happened for the express reason that he wanted to be able to get away from that place without being inundated with other pleas for help. Clark Kent is able to hold down the fort and be at the office phone, in case a call comes in from one of Superman's constituents demanding immediate, exclusive attention.

So the stage is set for the high point of the drama. The rescue is almost matter of fact, like a machine grinding away at its appointed task. Significantly Superman is a "man of steel." But the process that starts him on his way is most interesting. Kent receives the message. Then this same typical you-and-me sort of fellow, made of the dust of the earth, becomes our ideal, our dream, an image like God. Vulnerability puts on invulnerability. Now he is ready to serve his fellowman.

The implications are many. This whole book is something of a comment upon the theme of vulnerability and invulnerability. Let us here look at just two more points.

(1) *Morals*. What do we suppose Jesus meant when he said to take up our crosses and follow him? Each of us has a cross to bear in personal life. Some of us have several crosses. Jesus is telling us not to run away from them but to face them. Deal with them. Carry them. Shoulder our responsibilities even when the weight of them seems more than we can bear.

A few years ago campus demonstrators lost quite a bit of face with would-be sympathizers when they made amnesty a key issue of their movement. Whether one is for granting amnesty or not, it is a curious ethic that demands the freedom to rob the cookie jar without getting spanked. If demonstrators and war resisters are thought to be helping our country in the long run, the business of granting amnesty should be brought up and pushed by their supporters within the larger community. Their personal witness registers a flat zero on the scales of many when these demonstrators themselves riot for the sake of their own amnesty. An ethic that is not willing to be vulnerable is no ethic at all.

Yet for so many people the shape of what is right and wrong in our society is determined by "What will protect me from them?" At a public hearing in a suburban community a few years ago it was debated whether or not to bus inner-city children to the suburban school district. Since the intent of this completely voluntary program was racial exposure and sharing, it was assumed most of the inner-city kids would be black. The suburban community, needless to say, went into collective cardiac arrest. At the overflow hearing one man stood and shouted, "Them people is violent. If any of them tries anything with my kid, I'll blow their heads off!" Such is the mind of the fine upstanding citizen who structures his morality on the basis of self-protection and invulnerability. Incidentally, the speaker at that hearing sat down to a thunderous ovation.

The problem is no better solved by the liberal who is appalled at this kind of racism. The liberal of the living room variety has attended many a discussion group, read many a book, and is admittedly well informed. Alas, when the chips are down, liberalism too often ends where the liberal's driveway begins, while Christianity travels all the way to the cross.

Meanwhile, back at the protest, the demonstrator seems to have two messages to convey: (a) you (and the you may be the government, the school administration, the Establishment) are wrong; (b) you do something about it. Both of these messages are carefully worded to keep the hands of the demonstrators free from any responsibility. "Okay, Mr. President, give us peace. We have no idea how to do it. But then why should we? It is your job to come up with ways to find peace." Significantly these messages are couched in a new kind of medium. It is assumed that if enough people are in the protest, the individual will be protected. There just are not enough jails to house all of them, which may be a blessing.

Our purpose is not to pass judgment on any of these contemporary issues. The point is rather to expose the nonethic of avoiding vulnerability.

Clark Kent looks vulnerable. Though in fact he is steel, and we know it, he looks as though a solid left hook to his jaw would land him in the hospital, glasses shattered and chin smashed. It is necessary for the new image of invulnerability to emerge before action can take place.

Jesus of Nazareth went to his death because he did not wait for amnesty before challenging the spirits and ways of men. There is very little actual reform and human betterment that can take place as long as the disciples of Jesus Christ begin their discipleship by trying to protect themselves. We need a new and courageous beginning in the One who gave his life for us.

(2) *Commitment.* There is widespread misconception of what it means to come to Christ. People somehow assume they must be better people than they are before they can come to Jesus. It is as though we have

to go through a spiritual ritual like Clark Kent's in the storeroom, becoming a pious Superman, before God will have us.

Jesus must have had a great deal of sensitivity to this problem. He told a story of two men entering the temple. One of the men went to the altar and prayed, "Lord, thank you for making me so good." The other bowed humbly in the corner. "Lord, have mercy on me, a sinner." Jesus said that this latter man was heard by God. Some since have tried to manipulate the process, praying, "Lord have mercy on me, a sinner," while all the time thinking. "Aren't I great for praying the right prayer? Thank you, Lord, for making me so good." There was nothing phony about the man bowed in the corner. He meant every word of his prayer. He realized that to feel inadequate before God need not be cause for staying away from God. Rather, if shared honestly it can begin a new relationship.

Paul wrote what may be the Gospel in a nutshell: "while we were yet sinners Christ died for us (Rom. 5:8)." Christ did not wait for us to be ready for him. He gave his life for us, while we were sinners.

Essentially the refusal to give our life to Christ is a failure to trust God. Some of the reasons we hear for the refusal are righteous enough in their tone, but the message is the same. "I don't want to give my life to Christ, for fear that I might backslide later." "I don't want to give my life to Christ, because I am not really sincere." "I do not yet understand what this Christian faith is all about." All of these excuses are focused on one thing: the self. Of ourselves we will never be ready, or sufficiently sincere, or informed. While we were

unready, insincere, ignorant sinners, Christ died for us. The initiative for it all comes from God in his love. Why not trust him to lead us? Is he such an inept Lord that he would let us backslide right out of the faith? Will he not build our sincerity as he works in us? Will he not continually reveal himself to our understanding? Yes, we are spiritually vulnerable. All of us are. Jesus' disciples were. Christians through the long history of the church have been. We need not put on spiritual perfection to enter the kingdom. We need to get over ourselves, and what we can't do, and begin to trust God and what he can do.

There is a place in the kingdom for the Clark Kent in us all.

14

Can Anything Good Come out of Krypton?

We do not have the slightest inkling of how Kryptonians reproduce. The process has not been an urgent topic of speculation in medical circles or, for that matter, any other circles. All we know of Superman is that somehow he came into being on a planet far from earth. Krypton was about to explode when the young lad was hurled to earth to be the sole survivor of the lost species. According to the myth, he arrived while yet a boy and was adopted by white middle-class American parents who were soon to be astounded by the strength of their little darling.

The birth of Jesus is recorded in Matthew and Luke. The question that has long divided Christians is whether Mary really became pregnant through an act of the Holy Spirit or whether the church fabricated the story at a later date. Be that as it may, John's Gospel contains what may be the most important fact. The Word of God was made flesh. If Superman came to earth with all the qualities of the beyond, Jesus was born with the qualities of earth. He became a human being, a mortal. While the young Kryptonian was distressing his pediatrician by displaying a skin that could not be punctured by a hypodermic needle, the young Jesus was being rushed into Egypt so that the king would not be able to kill him.

The steel remained steel, but the Word was made flesh. On this basic fact lies a major difference between them.

There are quite a number of reasons why a dreamer is going to conjure up a Superman instead of a Jesus. A list of the reasons would merely reiterate what has gone before. Some thoughts, however, can be added.

A projected hero is a self-contained unit in and of himself. A genie does not need to rely on any other power. Neither does Superman. It is inconceivable that the mighty man in the blue tights and red cape would cry out for help while going about his work of rescuing Jimmy and Lois.

In trying to understand Jesus Christ, however, we are immediately brought up against the fact that he was not, in the flesh, a self-contained unit. He relied on something more. "God was in Christ (2 Cor. 5:19)." There is a dialogue in scripture between Jesus of Nazareth and God, his heavenly Father. Yes, Jesus is the meeting of God and man, as the early church fathers have told us. But he was very early in life aware of going about his heavenly Father's business. At his baptism, a voice from heaven made the announcement: "This is my beloved son, with whom I am well pleased (Matt. 3:17)." The fullness of God was in him. Those who saw him saw God, because the power of God, the Spirit of God, was in him and working through him.

It is somewhat out of fashion to suggest that Jesus was somehow dependent upon a power beyond earth. Sometimes the Jesus Movement has a hard time of knowing what to do with God the Father. The social action thrust has taken much of its impetus from the notion that God is no longer "out there" in the great beyond. In Christ he is in the world, in the market place or, as some are saying, "where the rubber hits the road."

Perhaps we need to take a fresh look at some old doctrines.

The importance of the virgin birth doctrine is that it is a way of saying that Jesus was somehow born of the Holy Spirit. He had the spirit in him. The importance of the doctrine of the trinity is that it reminds us Jesus is only a part of a larger Being at work in our world.

As Jesus approached his death, he went apart from his disciples to pray. He was not merely talking to himself. He was addressing an Other. We learn from the prayer that Jesus was upset, speaking to a Being who had a will independent of his own and yet a will that Jesus was able to take as his own as he faced the cross.

On the cross, Jesus quoted the book of Psalms, "My God, my God, why hast thou forsaken me? (Matt. 27:46; Mark 15:34)." He entered fully into the meaning of separation from God. Haven't we all felt that way from time to time, forsaken by God, far away from him? It can be a bitter experience. Why did God do this to me? What a comfort it is to remember that God's son suffered the same sense of separation for us. He himself faced apartness from God. He addressed the Other in the moment of his death. Inspired by the Spirit, he asked God to forgive his executioners. He gave his spirit to God. He died.

And then he rose from the dead. . . . No, that is not right. He did not rise from the dead. He *was raised* from the dead by God the Father. If Jesus were able to raise himself, obviously he would not have been dead and the resurrection would be a charade. He was very dead. Again, he was dependent upon a power from beyond, the Other, to restore his life.

Jesus is no projected hero, self-contained, self-sufficient. What he was able to do is all-sufficient for our salvation. But he did it only with the help of his heavenly Father. "God was in Christ reconciling the world to himself (2 Cor. 5:19)."

This opens the doorway to what may be the crux of comparison between projection and encounter. In some ways it harkens back to Chapter 8, in which we talked about not wanting to change at the fundamental levels of our being.

Superman runs on a power that is built into his body, much the same as red corpuscles are built into ours. His power is mystifying because it is so bound up within him that mortal men cannot comprehend it. There is no way that Jimmy Olsen could get an injection of Kryptonite and suddenly begin to leap over tall buildings. He has to be content to remain flesh and blood. There is a remoteness to the strength of the Man of Steel. No one shares in it. Superman must do all of his marvelous, awe-inspiring feats by himself, apart from human assistance.

What a different possibility is opened up in Jesus Christ! He was not running on some mysterious foreign element remote from us. God was in him, the same God who created all of us, the God who can also be at work in what we do.

The problem with an elaborate theology of the nature of Jesus is that it quite often creates a rather odd species that is neither God nor man. Jesus, then, is different from us, and we can convince ourselves intellectually that what he had at work in him would never be possible in us. We can go on just being plain old us. We can develop a spectator role before him, not unlike that of Herod in *Superstar,* who prances about the stage singing, "So you are the Christ, you're the great Jesus Christ. Prove to me that you're no fool, walk across my swimming pool." Jesus becomes an object for statues, miraculous stories, soupy pictures on the Sunday school wall. But he has no direct bearing on the way I might be able to live my life, and many would sigh, "Thank goodness!"

The Jesus we encounter on the pages of scripture, however, was another breed of man. He is tied to us in many ways. For openers, he lost his temper. He cried. He got thirsty and hungry. He got tired. "The Word became flesh (John 1:14)." He showed us in his life what our life can be all about.

We need always remember, before going further, that there is a certain arrogance to which we might rather easily fall victim here. You and I are not Jesus. Much the same as little boys and girls dream of Superman, there are others who have dreamed of being Jesus, wondering if they are to grow up to be the Second

Coming. Jesus was the *only* begotten son of God. That means in plain English, or in plain Latin, or in plain Greek, or however you write it, that we are not the begotten sons and daughters of God. Sometimes, reading modern ethics, I get the impression that many forget that fact and live as though they were Jesus, taking what they think were the liberties Jesus took with the law and with respected authorities.

The point is not at all to suggest that we can become Jesus. The point is to be made aware that we can be Christlike in our living. We may not be the begotten sons of God. But because of Jesus Christ we can become children of God, born of the Spirit. In the Presbyterian liturgy of baptism are the words, "See what love the Father has given to us that we should be called children of God, and so we are."

Jesus had a very familiar term that he used in addressing God. He called him "Abba," which in the Aramaic literally meant "Dad." It was a term of affection and closeness. To those who insisted upon the remoteness of God, it was a term of some irreverence. It was a term indicative of a new kind of relationship with the Other, who is not a remote Kryptonian but One with whom we can be intimate. When Jesus taught his disciples to pray, he began the prayer, "Our Abba." The intimacy that he knew with his heavenly Father we too can know, as we pray together, as his family.

The power of God that was so fully present in the only begotten son of the Father can be present in you and in me. One need only look around today at the tremendous miracles being performed by people of faith. The hungry are fed. The blind receive their sight.

The sick are healed. Observing all of these thrilling happenings, I am personally struck by the integrity of the Christlike people through whom the miracles have occurred. They all insist that they deserve no credit. "I am nothing," they say. "It is God working through me." That God who worked so completely in Jesus Christ can work through the body of Christ today.

The task is to let him. The question of discipleship is not always one of asking how we can be more worthy, more deserving of God's love. Sometimes, in fact most times, it is a question of how we can be less in the way of God's will. The task of discipleship is getting our pride, our lack of trust, our selfish desires out of the way, so that we can be open to the power of God.

God can do unbelievable things through us if we will open ourselves wide to him and let him go to work using us for his glory.

Superman could die.

What a frightening thought that was for us kids, perched on the edges of our fourteen-cent seats at the Saturday matinee. We had not yet figured out that the writers of the serial were not about to kill off their bread and butter. Rather it was sheer faith in our hero's ability somehow to pull through that kept us going.

I recall one episode where Superman was lowered down a conveyor belt into a room filled with poisonous gas (kryptonite gas, I now suppose). He fell off the end of the conveyor belt to the floor, where he lay for some time. Then, with what little strength he had left, he dragged himself across the cement floor a few yards and . . . fell . . . lifeless. You could have heard a piano drop, the theater noise had quieted down so much. It looked as though our champion was a goner.

But then, as if to reverse the script, came the sound of a *whoosh* of wind. Jimmy had opened a window, and the kryptonite gas escaped. Fresh air was let in. Superman moved. He was alive. Now you could not hear a piano drop. He got up, still a bit woozy, wobbly on his legs, and staggered to the window. "Thanks, Jimmy." (Superman thanks people, if they do not often thank him.) Jimmy helped him through the window. In a moment he was flying again. Our hero was flying again!

Moments like that are not a common part of the script. But they do occur. Superman could die, and we know it. Of course any sophisticated post-teenybopper knows that he will not. There is a message there. Those genies that came out of lanterns had one weakness: They were limited to three tricks. How much better is a projected hero whose bag of tricks is everlasting! Superman, like old man river, just keeps rolling along.

Furthermore, he has built into him a quite nonscary way of dying. If he could die of a coronary, or cancer, or a car accident, that might be a bit too close to us and would make us uneasy. But what is more harmless than kryptonite? I knew, as a kid, that I could touch it, smell it, even taste it, and have no harmful side effects. Only Superman is jeopardized by this weird element, which apparently came to earth at the time of the explosion of that faraway planet. In fact when Superman even gets near the stuff, he keels over. A prolonged exposure would be fatal. Jimmy probably rescued Superman just in time, opening that window and letting the gas escape, while he himself was in absolutely no danger.

Death, as far as Superman is concerned, is quite different from anything we know or fear from our own experience.

But Jesus died. As we will die. Instead of being a part of the drama hidden by the writers, the death of Jesus is the major event in the four narratives of his life. No kryptonite was found to do him in. All that was required was a cross. In those days crucifixion was the most horrible way to die, hung up there for all to see, as gradually your strength and breath left you. Sometimes a single spike was driven into the ground, with the victim hung up looking like a capital I. Other times a capital X was used, with two crossing stakes driven into the ground. Jesus was hung up on a T, probably with the crossbar lowered a bit from the top.

Usually a person would hang on a cross for some time, perhaps even days, before dying. To add to the insult, victims were often stripped naked. The two thieves on either side of Jesus may have been there many hours before the third cross was dropped into place. As we know, there was not enough time for the crucifixion to do its work. The legs of the two thieves had to be broken. There is speculation as to whether Jesus was already dead when the spear entered his side or whether that killed him. Being religious people, the crowds did not allow bodies to hang on a cross during the sabbath, so Jesus and his two fellow victims were taken down, dead.

This descriptive material is included to illustrate the fact that Jesus died in a way we could die. Fortunately we are past the day of crucifixion. Execution and murder are not behind us, by any means, but at least we have changed our technique. Jesus died because he was killed by people, who used a method of murder that would work quite nicely on us.

It is pathetically humorous to hear people try to work their way around this fact. "Jesus," they say, "could have got himself off the cross at any time." When the soldiers stood at the foot of the cross and taunted our Lord to save himself, a common notion is to interpret that moment as one of great self-control on Jesus' part. Could he have jumped down from the cross and smashed those stupid soldiers? Or was that merely the wish of Jewish nationals who wanted him to be a messiah? Or is it the wish of those of us who want him to be something different from us?

Obviously God is free to get anyone out of a tight jam. Certainly he could have freed all three victims from their crosses. But such random speculating misses the key point. Jesus had made his decision to obey while he was kneeling at prayer in the Garden of Gethsemane. The decision was made before the cross. In the garden he offered the prayer, "Not as I will, but as thou wilt (Matt. 26:39)." Jesus the man was then captured. Jesus the man, who had prayer just a few moments before that he wanted the cup to pass from him, was led away toward his death. Are we to assume that there was a phone booth somewhere between Gethsemane and Golgotha into which Jesus slipped and emerged as a Superman who would hang there on the cross, cleverly disguised as a helpless man but really ready to pounce on his enemies? That is nonsense. The Word became flesh. Jesus was a man, albeit a man in whom the power of God was at work. But the man who hung there on the cross was dying our death, not some make-believe charade of it.

The point of identification between us and Christ is on that cross. Let us not miss that point by insisting Jesus was really Superman. The greatest fear any of us has is the fear of dying. What lies beyond it? What will it be like? If I die, will that be it, or is there more? We know that no matter where we live, how well we take care of ourselves, death is inevitably going to meet us.

When the only begotten son of God came to earth he met us at the point of our ultimate question—death. The psalmist, like so many Old Testament writers, caught a glimmer of what was to come. "Even though I walk through the valley of the shadow of death, I fear no evil, for thou art with me (Ps. 23:4)." Of one thing we can be certain. As death rears its ugly head, we are not alone. Jesus is there. He has been through it. He is our companion, leading us into the valley and through it.

Because he died as we will die, Jesus is able to do for us what Superman can never do. Thanks be to God who has given us the victory through our Lord Jesus Christ. Jesus was raised from the dead. He was dead and now he is alive. While all of the scripts for the Superman comic books, radio plays, and TV shows have been written on the premise that the Man of Steel must not die, every word of the New Testament was written *after* Jesus had already died and been raised to new life. The projection of Superman tries to sustain the old life. In Christ we encounter the new life.

In his first letter to the Corinthian church, Paul wrote, "If for this life only we have hoped in Christ, we are of all men most to be pitied (1 Cor. 15:19)." Poor Lois and Jimmy. They do not have hope in Superman beyond this earthly life. All their hero can do is prolong what now is, with all of its fears and anxieties. The fundamental question of life remains unanswered. It is impossible for the projector to answer the question of his own life. We cannot, by dreaming, find the answer to the question about death. It has to come to us from an Other who encounters us from the perspective of having conquered death.

There are quite a number of ways in which modern thinkers are trying to put down the resurrection. Some suggest that there was a plot afoot to make it look as if Jesus had died when in fact he had not. Others suggest that the plot aborted when Jesus died anyway, but that his followers kept the plot going by imagining him. Still others are of the opinion that when he died Jesus of Nazareth stayed dead. His spirit was then resurrected in the form of the early church.

Paul puts it best. "Now if Christ is preached as raised from the dead, how can some of you say that there is no resurrection? (1 Cor. 15:12)." It would seem that we are really getting caught up in our own mental messes when in the name of Christian scholarship we deny the resurrection.

What was it that reunited the disciples? What turned that crew of frightened people into a spiritual army that changed human history? What changed their deep grief into lasting hope? Shall we say they remembered a plot? Shall we say they saw a mirage?

Shall we say they decided by the power of the Spirit to become a church? All of these seem insufficient. The turnabout in the lives of those people came when they encountered the risen Christ. John makes a point of it in the way he tells the story of Thomas, the disciple not with the others when the risen Lord first appeared to them. Thomas was a cool customer, not tricked easily. He was a questioner, a curious-minded chap. Some call him a doubter. Those who study what little we know of him are impressed by how scientific he was in his approach to things that matter. He was led back to the room, and he saw Jesus. He fell on his knees. "My Lord and my God! (John 20:28)" he exclaimed.

Thomas was face to face with the answer to life's most nagging question. There stood the man who had died, the man who had been humiliated, tortured, the man who had breathed his last. Thomas like all the others thought that, for better or for worse, Jesus was in the beyond, whatever that meant. But now he was back. Not only had he been raised to new life, he was back to let others in on it.

The reason for coming back is to show others the way. Jesus did not return to torment his followers by saying, Look what happened to me; it won't happen to you. He was back to say, It can happen to you, too. Like the college student visiting his high school, showing the kids that one of their own can make it: It can happen to you, too. The astronaut, the soldier, the athlete returning to the ghetto—Jesus returned to his people to say, It can happen to you. Believe me.

Some years ago there was a tremendous fascination

with an experiment in hypnosis. A lady was asked to recount the events of her earliest years, which she did with remarkable clarity. At this point the doctors decided to take the big step and ask her to describe what it was like years before she was born. To their amazement, she did, telling of a little girl in Ireland by the name of Bridie Murphy. The interest over this event was phenomenal. Did we have here a clue to what life was like beyond the confines of the beginning and the end of the earthly journey? Do we come back as someone else? But it turned out that there were problems with the Bridie Murphy story.

What difference does it make? Why should we get so fascinated chasing after these false answers? We already have the answer in Jesus Christ. When we die, we are very dead, just as Jesus was dead. But God raises the new Body of Christ. We are raised from the dead to be with our heavenly Father. That is something we cannot project, or even imagine. It is something we encounter.

15

Up, Up, and Away!

While I was in college a tragedy occurred. George Reeves, who played the part of Superman in the TV series, was found dead.

Now quite a bit can be said of my classmates, both positively and negatively. Reverence for the dead and dying, however, was not their long suit. A well-known figure would be reported on his or her deathbed, and students would be making bets as to the exact day—in the more elaborate booking circles, it was down to the hour—at which the person might die. Needless to say, the tragic death of Mr. Reeves did not go without some pungent pieces of Princeton profundity.

"Superman is dead!" they cried. In the library, in the dorm, by the Good Humor truck—"Superman is dead!" It was a remark of sarcastic wit making its own point, as we college boys did in those days, quite relevant to the age in which it was uttered. The absurdity of a Man of Steel, strange visitor from another planet, able to leap tall buildings in a single bound! What saps we had been as little kids, being conned into worshiping

that steel clown! Now we had a chance to laugh at our
past, our ridiculous dreams, and to assert, in however
trivial a way, our emancipation from childhood. Any-
how, the Untouchables and Rocky the Flying Squirrel
were better watching anyway. So I laughed along with
them. "Superman is dead!"

With a diploma under my arm, I crossed the street
to what university students call "the angel factory,"
more widely known as a theological seminary. To my
dismay, I discovered in mid-stream that another
tragedy had supposedly occurred. I don't recall where I
was when I first got the news, or even how I took it.
For some reason it never shook me much. "God is
dead," they were saying. In the library, in the dormi-
tory, by the Good Humor truck, even on the cover of
Time—"God is dead."

Oddly, it felt a lot like George Reeves revisited. All
those seminary students were getting in their licks
against the God of their Sunday school teachers, their
youth fellowship leaders, even their ministers. It was
a declaration of manhood, an emancipation from
"their God so that now we can find our own." Many
were saying that the old "pie-in-the-sky" God had to
die so that the real "in the marketplace" God could be
discovered. Others were simply laughing at the whole
idea of God as a relic from their childhood that had
been outgrown.

The sixties were ripe for this sort of thing. The early
years of the decade set the pace. John Kennedy was
elected President in 1960. His administration was characterized by the word he uttered so often in his Boston
twang, "Vigah." It was a vigorous time. The confident

hope was that through human brains, compassion, and technology any problem could be solved anywhere. Mr. Kennedy challenged science to go to the moon in ten years. It was a seemingly impossible target that was nonetheless hit within the decade. Many of the goals of the Kennedy administration were achieved, including some of the most far-reaching pieces of civil rights legislation (passed primarily under Lyndon Johnson). It was said that some of the Kennedy staff were hungry for crises so that they could leap in and apply their know-how to work out a solution. From Selma to Saigon, they searched. It was a day and age when the brilliant minds of our nation were stretching, perhaps as never before—from Cape Canaveral where the rocket program was growing by leaps and firings to California where scientists were inviting young college students to act as guinea pigs for experiments with a new wonder drug, LSD. If we need a solution, man can find it. If we find something that works, use it. Never have we had such an orgy of self-confidence. "Man can do all things through man."

The shock of November 22, 1963, was doubly difficult. It killed our leader, with whom Americans felt an incredibly close relationship, and left a brave widow and a little boy saluting his father's coffin. It also put a needle right in the middle of our great big balloon. The trouble with hope is that it leads so easily to despair if it is vested in the wrong object. Man worshiping man is a hope doomed sooner or later to failure. The young people making headlines by joining the Peace Corps were, in just a few years, making headlines by taking over college buildings and protesting at the 1968 Democratic convention. The black people marching to Washington to hear Dr. Martin Luther King speak were, in just a short time, to be rioting in the ghettos. Dr. King himself would die of an assassin's bullet. Hope became despair.

But we are getting ahead of ourselves. In those glory years of the sixties, when we still assumed that man left to himself could solve all of his own problems, we obviously had no need for beings like Superman and God. Superman went because we did not need to project dream heroes. We had a fine enough dream going on right in the good old United States.

God went for more complicated reasons. The projected god of popular religion died as the Man of Steel died. People did not need to dream of him any more. Others found that their church was dying because it was worshiping a God who was interested in nothing but social action. Still others found it a nuisance and quite unnecessary to encounter an Other in a time like this.

In the late sixties, I considered writing about the Superman series and was told quite flatly that it was too late. "Why bother?" I was told. "Who ever thinks of Superman these days? He is a thing of the past." I got the same impression in the seminary, where God was held up in much the same way. What was left of him was out in the marketplace, or making human life more human, whatever that means.

Dietrich Bonhoeffer was the theologian of the hour. As with so many great minds, it is sometimes hard to separate what Bonhoeffer was actually saying from what his disciples insist he was trying to say. But two quotes are germane. He wrote "God is no longer necessary as a working hypothesis." More popular among us post-adolescents was the ditty, "Man has come of age." I am not certain whether Bonhoeffer really believed these little gems as statements of fact or if he had the wisdom to believe that this was merely the way modern man felt about himself. Since Bonhoeffer was held captive in a Nazi prison and was finally hanged, I find it hard to imagine that he really meant that man had come of age, though I find it quite within the bounds of common sense for him to discern man as thinking himself to be of age. Why else the nonsense of Hitler?

The Anglican bishop John A. T. Robinson took the writings of Bonhoeffer, Paul Tillich, and Rudolf Bultmann and wrote the theology of the sixties in a little book entitled *Honest to God*. Quite frankly, I found the book helpful. The gist of what the bishop was saying is that God is right here in the midst of human life, not at all an Other as our Sunday school teachers tried to tell us. It was a helpful balance for a faith too much vested in the supernatural. A seminary student coming out of the angel factory in the mid-sixties might well have chosen a funeral oration for God as his first sermon and an offering up of mankind as the hope of the world for his second. After that he would probably leave his pulpit and become a social worker.

God and Superman were no longer necessary as working hypotheses. It is not without significance that when people begin to celebrate their own greatness they project neither comic-strip heroes nor pop-religion gods. At the same time they have an aversion to encountering the Other. One might be willing to applaud for theological reasons the demise of pop religion. But the record is that genuine encounter too often goes down with it. Pop religion is, after all, the manifestation of the fact that people are hungry. They are searching for something, a meaning, a directive, a fullness to life. The longing has been lodged in inadequate places. Pop religion is not enough. It is a perversion of the real encounter. But a wise reaper sees it as a sign that at least a harvest is possible.

The problem of the great celebration of *us* that characterized the sixties is that it was a dead-end street. Have we ever had such high hopes throw us to such low depths? Confident that the goodness of man could do all, heralding the good news that it no longer matters what a man's religion is, snubbing the pre-intellectual fifties—we ended up in what one commentator called a national nervous breakdown. Even the great dream of people working together as brothers and sisters ended in a fiasco as young were set against old, black against white, poor against rich, female against male. Admittedly, some of this is due to the emergence of groups too long held down, only now getting into the decision-making process. I could rest comfortably with that were it not for the bitterness, the anger and despair and hopelessness, that characterizes it all.

I leave it to historians in future decades to tell us exactly when the tide turned. At some point it began slowly to dawn that we had been traveling down the wrong path. Though we hate to admit it, the redneck had been at least half right. You cannot make people get along with each other by force of law. We cannot solve our problems on our own. Maybe it was Vietnam.

Maybe it was civil disobedience. Maybe it was crime. Maybe it was drugs. Maybe it was the gradual awareness by the silent majority that those blasted hippies had a point to their antics. Whatever the cause, there has been a death to the death-of-Superman and death-of-God movements. For a time it has been hard to tell if it is merely a death of death or in fact a resurrection.

It now looks as though something new has arisen and is very much at work in our world. Evangelism is no longer a dirty word. We can talk about Bible study, and kids will not get ill. Billy Graham can bring a crusade to town, and the established church will not try to block it; in fact they will work with it. It is a new day.

Again the Superman model is helpful. We find in the ways the Man of Steel has returned that people are not yet ready to leap back into the style of the forties and fifties. He is not appearing through his former media. Rather his presence is more diffuse. He is into a little bit of everything: commercials, cocktail party banter, costumes at dress-up time.

So with God. Established religion is still in trouble. The main denominations of the postwar years are not booming. The mad dash to erect new edifices has turned rather abruptly into concern about how to pay for the ones we have already built and are now stuck with. Church attendance and membership have tapered off, and opinion surveys reveal that the authority of the church has tumbled.

The renewed or revived spirit blowing across Christendom has not caused a flood of saints to inundate the established churches, any more than the return of Superman is sending us all back to our radios and comic-book shelves. Instead we see the Spirit at work in new forms. If the main-line denominations are barely holding their own, the sects are booming; groups whose names were unheard of a decade ago are constantly starting new churches or putting additions on the ones they have. Some might raise their eyebrows at this practice, except that the sects are filling those buildings almost as soon as they complete them and are paying off the mortgage promptly.

The Spirit is at work in living rooms, on street corners, on college campuses. (Who would have thought it in 1968?) We are discovering that a new openness has emerged between the established church and the extra-ecclesiastical ministries. Youth organizations like Young Life or Campus Crusade were at first vigorously opposed by clergymen who were afraid that these outfits would rob them of their youth groups. Gradually, in the late sixties these churchmen faced two realities: (1) They did not have youth groups anyway, and (2) parents were calling up, frantic, wanting guidance about how to get Junior off drugs. The clergyman had no answer to that, and he could see that youth movements, leading kids to Christ, did have an answer.

We are living in a great time. The Spirit is at work in many wonderful ways. Maybe we are like alcoholics who need to hit bottom before we are willing or able to ask for help. In Western civilization we are beginning to ask and God is answering. We are returning in faith to God, to Jesus, to religion.

This book has been written with the firm conviction that now is the time to open ourselves to the Other, as he comes to us in scripture and in Jesus Christ. It is time to receive him on his terms, rather than ours. We have had enough of our terms in recent years. Now it is his turn.

In this period when people are searching, when people are hungry, in this time when my phone, like that of many other clergymen, is ringing with lives looking for something—we are in the presence of great danger and great possibility. People are projecting again. The god that is being bandied about by many today is a superficial figment of human wishes and dreams. The god of pop religion, the god of projection, is back. But that in itself does not scare me. It means that the time is right. People are ready for an encounter with the living God, the Other, who can remake the lives of us all.